PICTURES of EVERYTHING
ABSTRACT PAINTING NOW

EILEEN BOXER   GREG BRICKEY   STEPHEN CIMINI   ROBYN ELLENBOGEN   ROBIN FELD
GLENN   GARVER   ELIZABETH   GILFILEN   MARIA   PAVLOVSKA   RAYMOND   SAA

CURATED BY JAMES PUSTORINO

Victory Hall DRAWING ROOMS

CONTENTS

EILEEN BOXER

GLENN GARVER

GREG BRICKEY

STEPHEN CIMINI

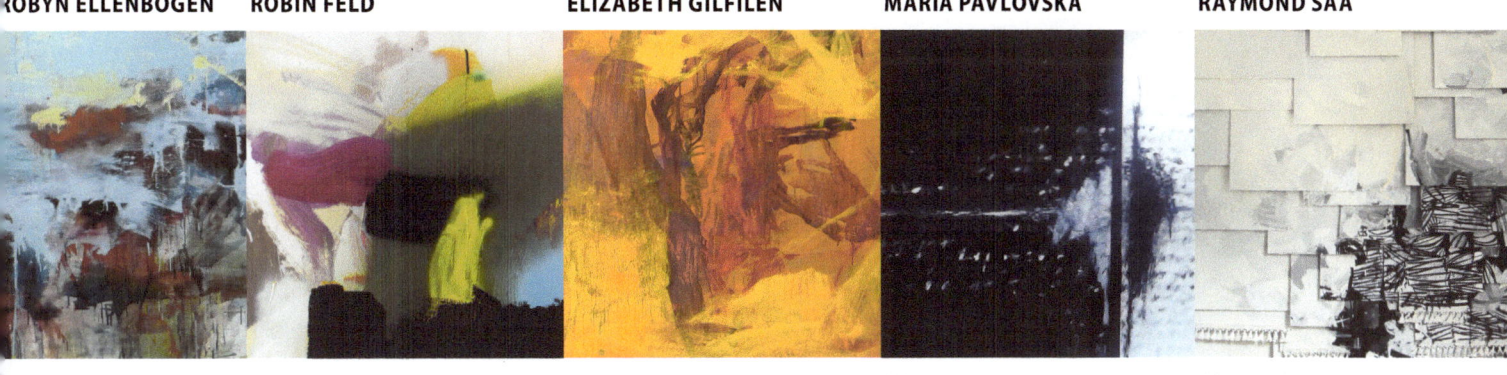

Victory Hall DRAWING ROOMS is a contemporary art center for drawing, painting, and print located in downtown Jersey City, featuring continually developing exhibitions of exciting new works by artists in the NY/NJ area. With ten rooms of exhibition space, year round exhibits and convenient gallery hours, we create opportunities for artists to connect with their community and create possibilities for artist interaction, art sales, and attention from curators and the press on a consistent basis.

Visit us at www.drawingrooms.org

INTRODUCTION

Pictures of Nothing or Pictures of Everything? Does abstract art empty out content and subject matter, or does it pile on those concepts in order to make a painting that says even more than the thousand words a picture is supposed to have assigned to it? People have been debating the simplicity or complexity of abstract painting for more than a hundred years, and continue to be moved by new abstract works in one way or another, both emotionally and intellectually.

For our Spring 2014 exhibition, DRAWING ROOMS gathers nine artists working in the NY/NJ area who have taken on the task of exploring and re-inventing abstract painting to make their own personal, visual statement.

Several years ago Kirk Varnedoe, former Curator at the Museum of Modern Art, delivered an important series of lectures about Abstract art since the 1950s called *Pictures of Nothing*. Starting with the famous drip paintings by Jackson Pollock, he described how abstract painting moved from active, expressive imagery to the more rarefied "empty" forms of minimal art and beyond. But what has happened since then? When we look around, much of the abstraction being made now seems full of content: ideas, emotion, form, color, drawing —and sometimes even images that seem to be appearing or disappearing. In this exhibition we take a look at what is going on currently in the world of abstract art through the contributions of these artists, and the statement it suggests recalls the title of one of our exhibiting artist's paintings: *Everything Included*.

JAMES PUSTORINO
Director, Victory Hall DRAWING ROOMS

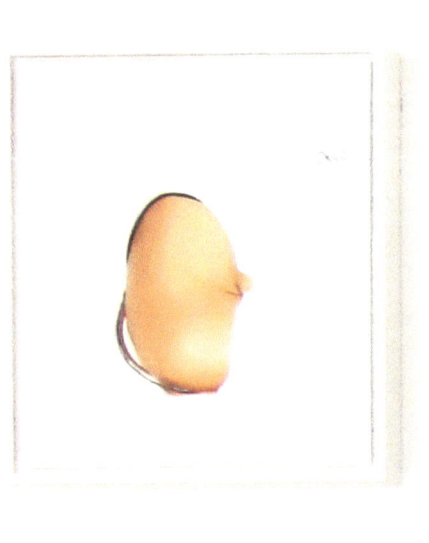
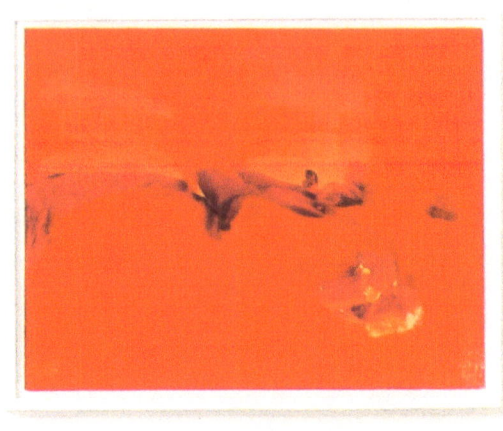
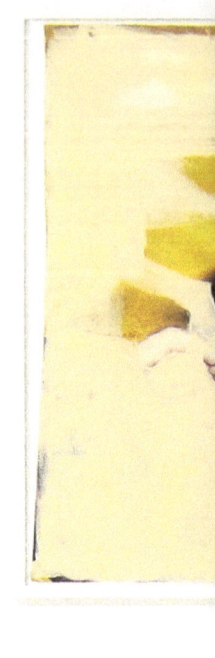
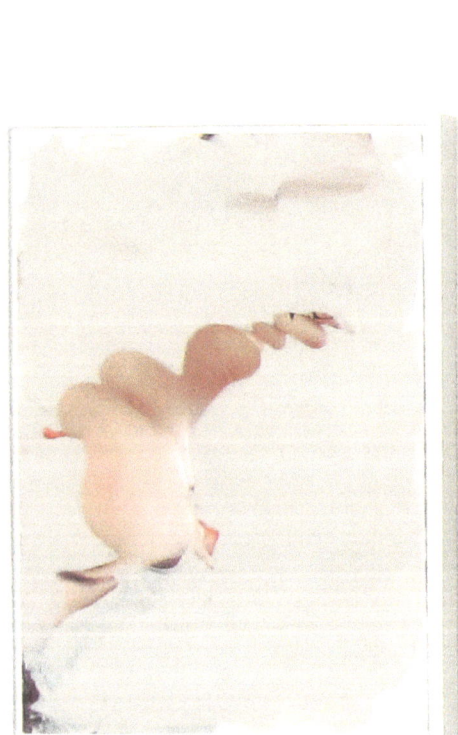
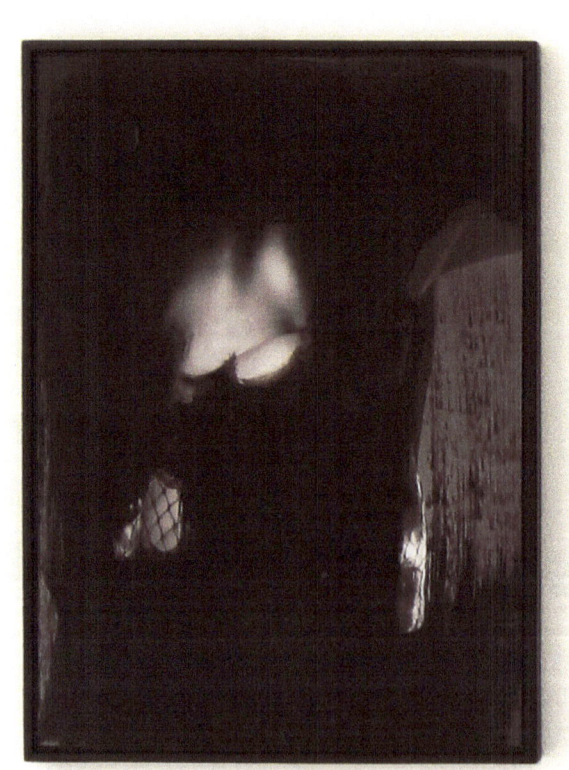
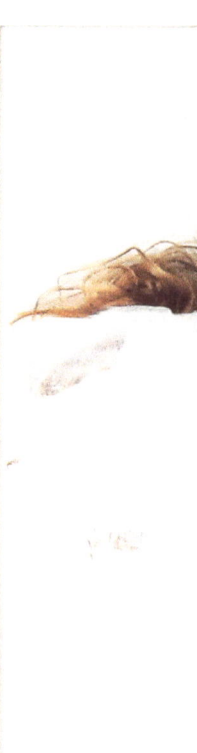

EILEEN BOXER was born in Brooklyn, New York, and grew up in Hong Kong. She studied Fine Art as an undergraduate from Boston University, and holds a BFA in communication arts from Parsons. In addition, she has pursued graduate studies in Fine Arts at SVA and Pratt. Well established as a graphic and book designer for the art and museum world, Ms Boxer has intermittently maintained a studio practice for the past 30 years.

"Photographs represent our three dimensional environment in two dimensions, allowing us to flatten and find the conversation of form and color of seemingly completely disconnected elements. I see these relationships everywhere in front of me—it is how I see. With paint, I find something underneath.

These painted photographs are about desire, but at the same time they're about repulsion. They're about something beautiful and haunting. I wanted something that was as restricted as early renaissance painting, but also the freedom and passion of surrealism. These things that pull against one another like, "yes no, yes no"—this tug of war—I want less, I want more." —EB

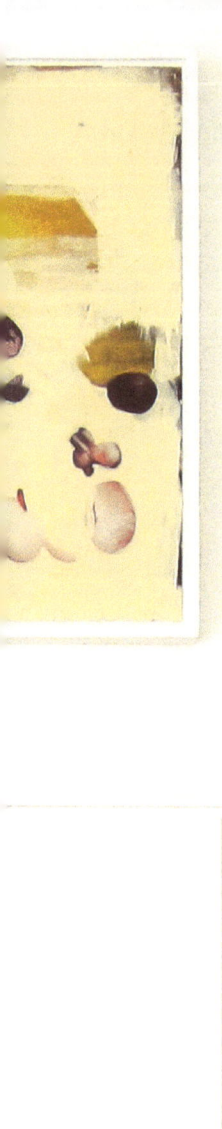
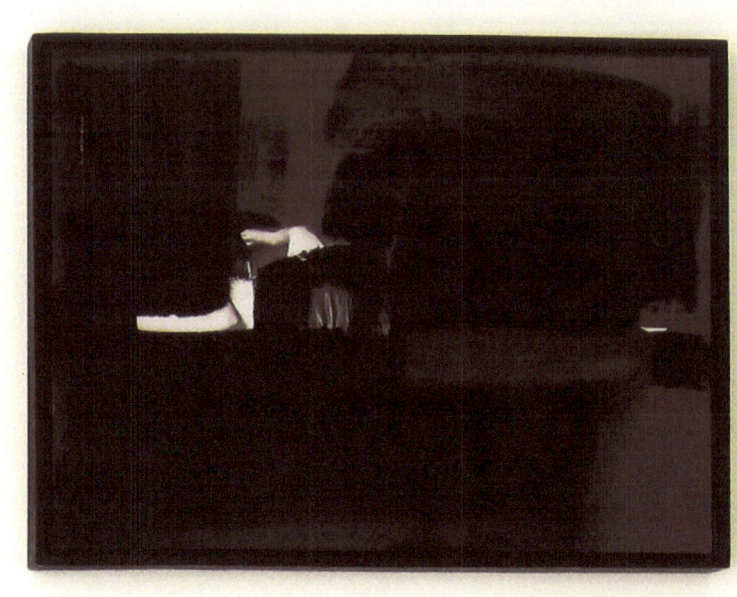
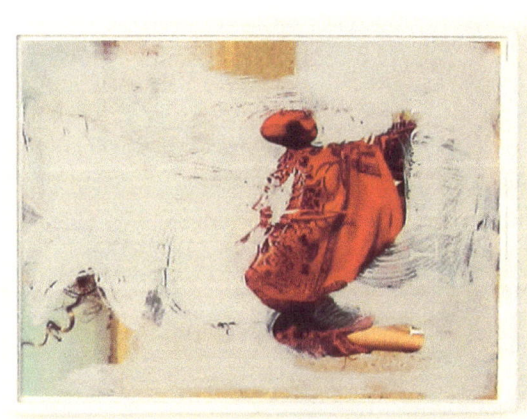
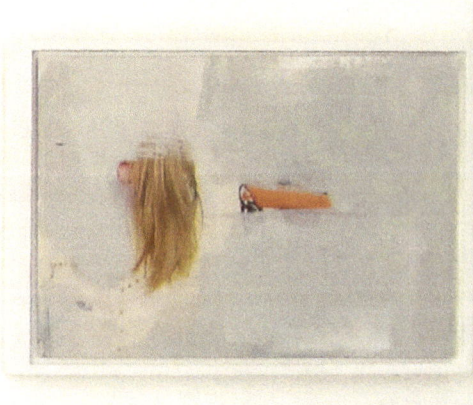
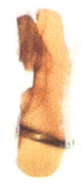
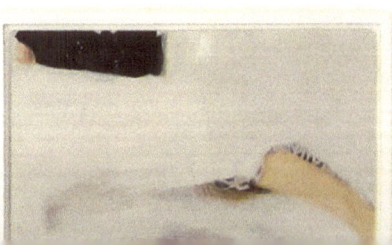
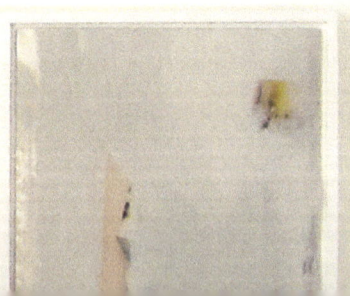

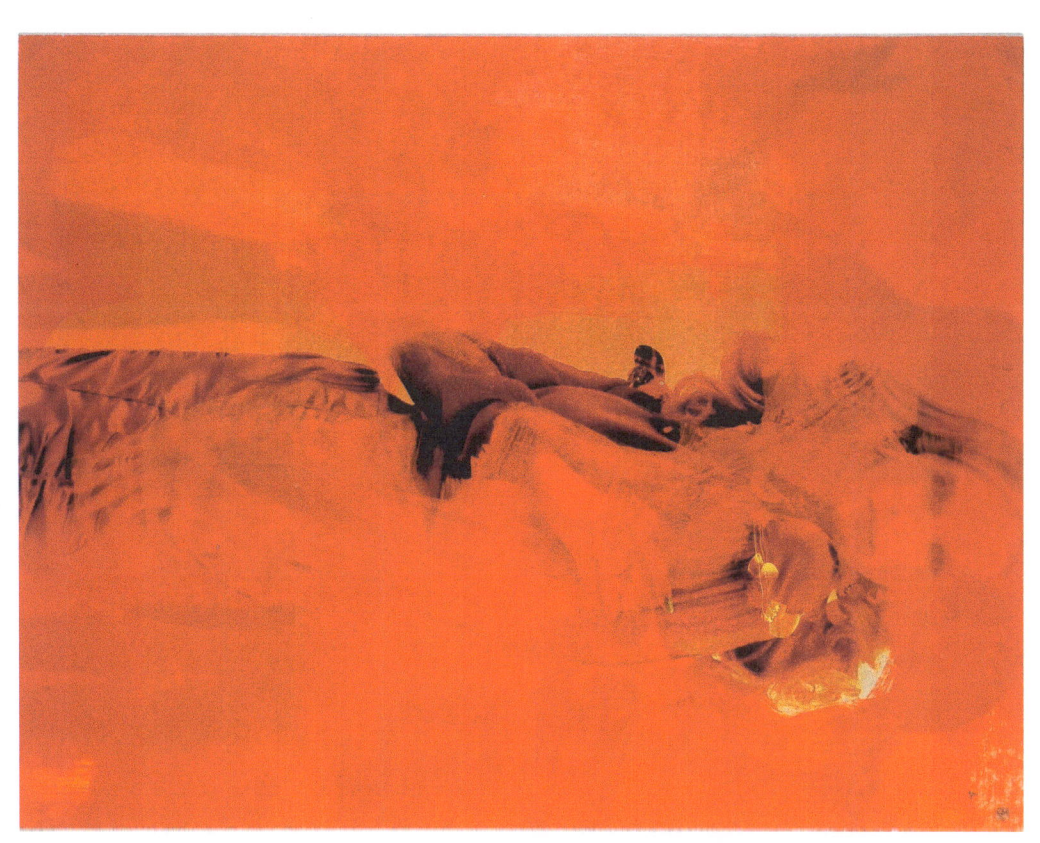

UNTITLED [353], 2013 ACRYLIC ON MAGAZINE PAGE. FRAME (NOT SHOWN): 8 × 10.25 IN. IMAGE: 7.12 × 9.5 IN.

[FROM UPPER LEFT] UNTITLED 354, 353, 351 (PARTIAL), 46-VAN TRESS, 363, 40, 2012–13
ACRYLIC ON MAGAZINE PAGE. VARIOUS SIZES, ALL MOUNTED WITH HANDMADE FRAMES BY THE ARTIST

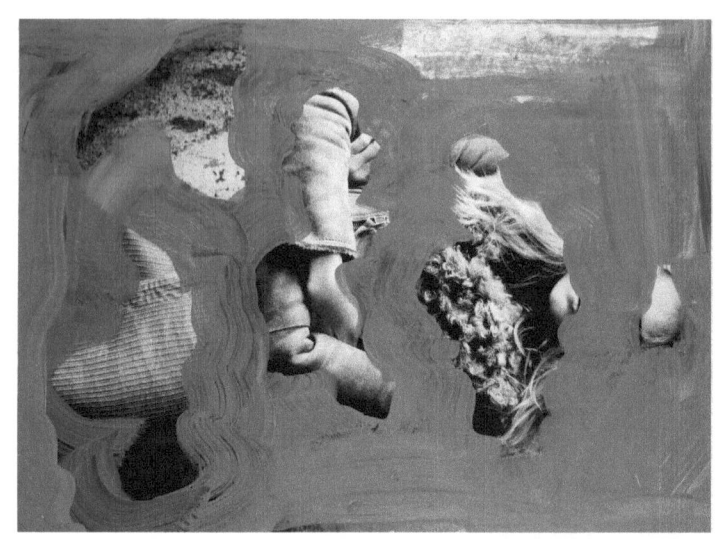

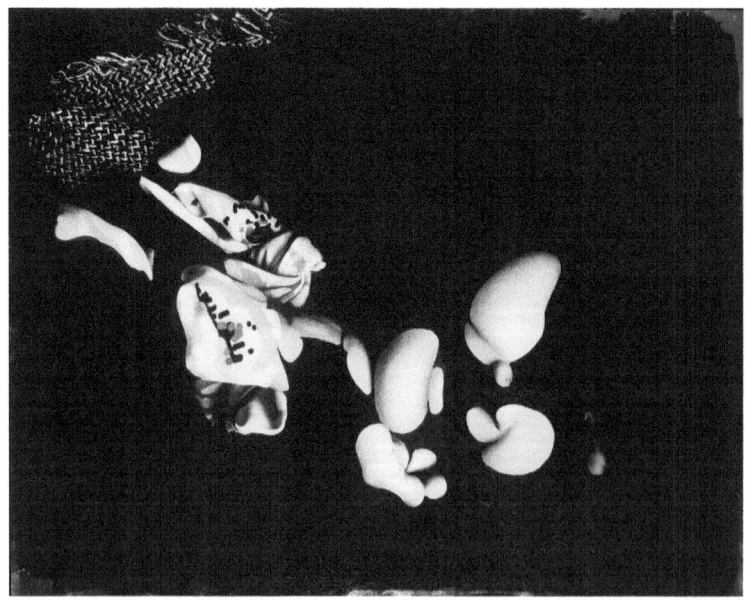

[TOP] UNTITLED [352], 2013 ACRYLIC ON MAGAZINE PAGE. FRAME (NOT SHOWN): 8.12 × 11 IN. IMAGE: 7.4 × 10.25 IN.

[TOP] UNTITLED [361], 2012 ACRYLIC ON MAGAZINE PAGE. FRAME (NOT SHOWN): 8.75 × 11 IN. IMAGE: 8 × 10.4 IN.

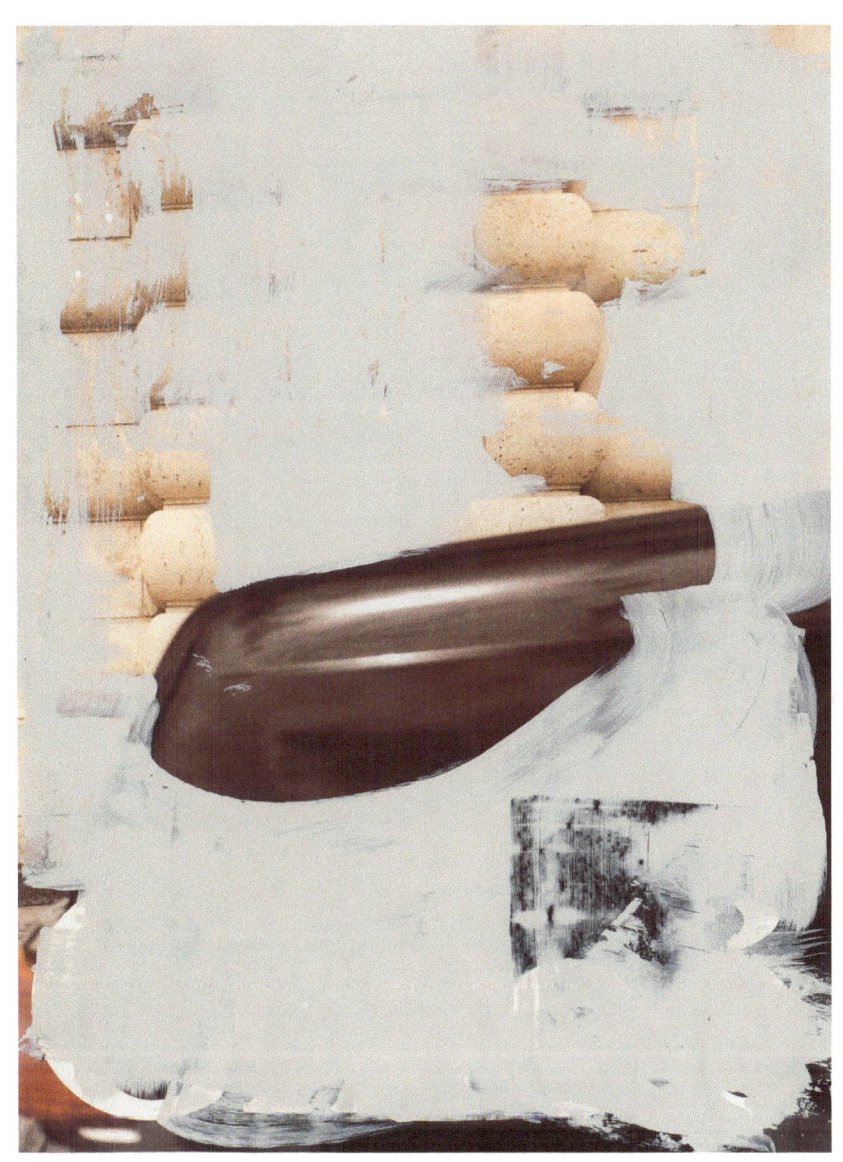

UNTITLED [349], 2012 ACRYLIC ON MAGAZINE PAGE. FRAME (NOT SHOWN): 12.125 × 9.5 IN. IMAGE: 11.4 × 8.75 IN.

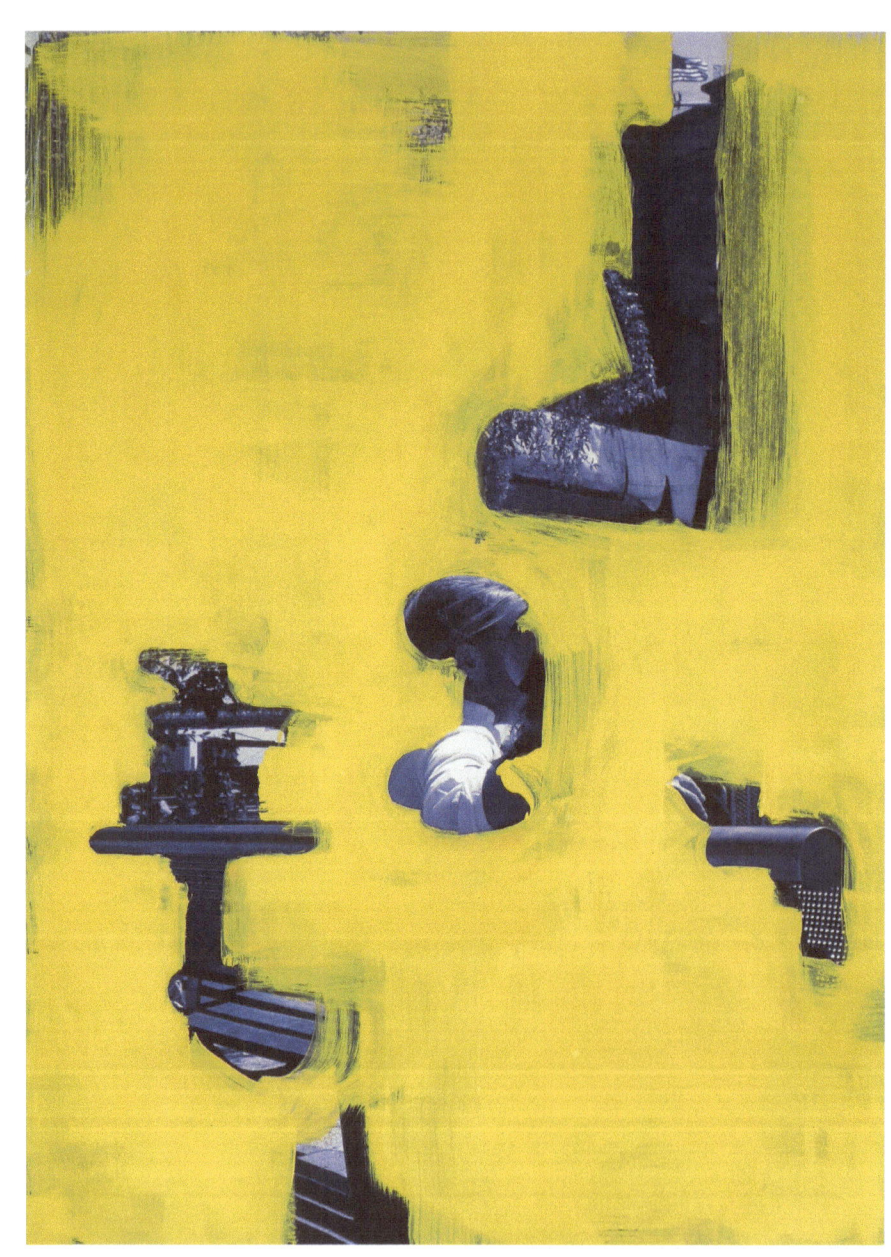

MADRIGAL 031, 2012 ACRYLIC ON MAGAZINE PAGE ON BOARD, 20.5 × 15 IN.

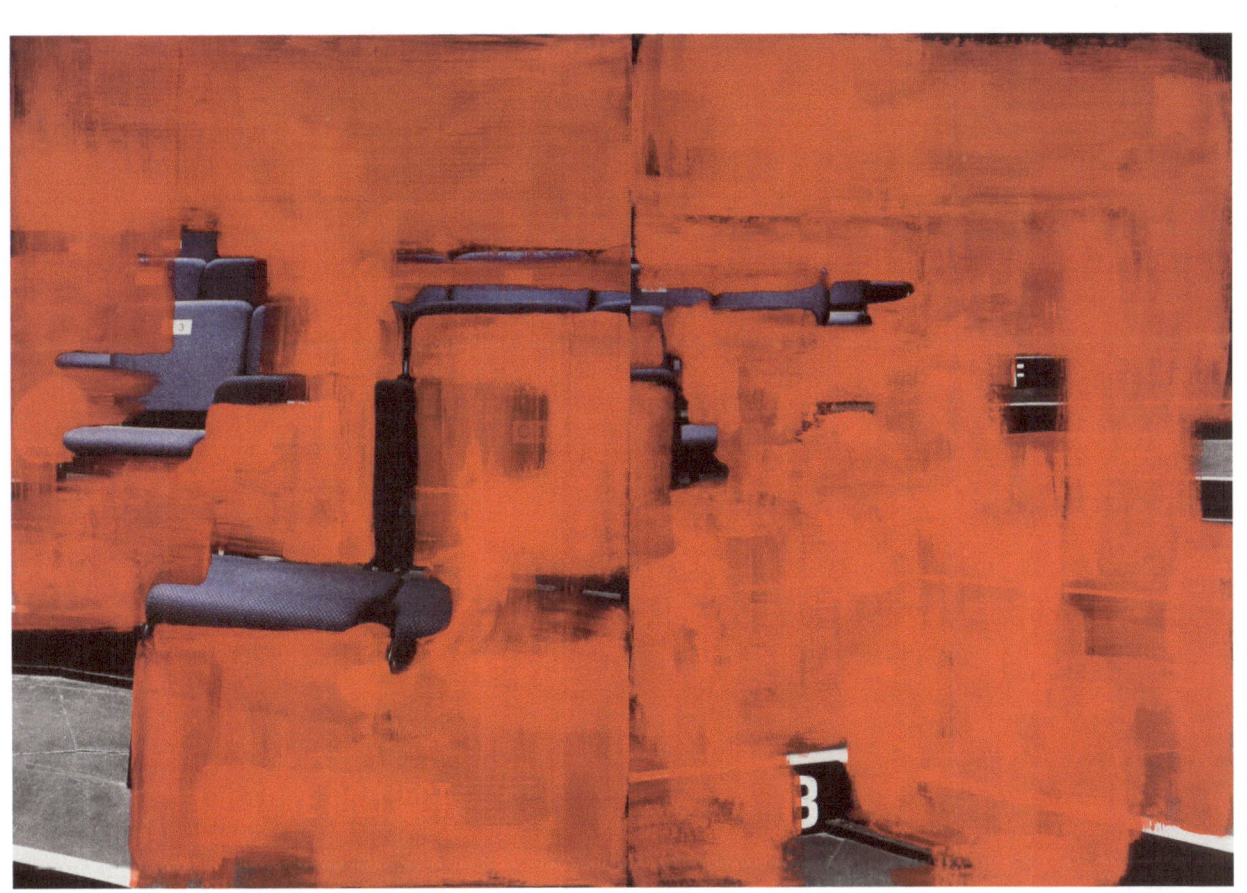

MADRIGAL 06, 2012 ACRYLIC ON MAGAZINE PAGE ON BOARD, DIPTYCH 20.5 × 30 IN.

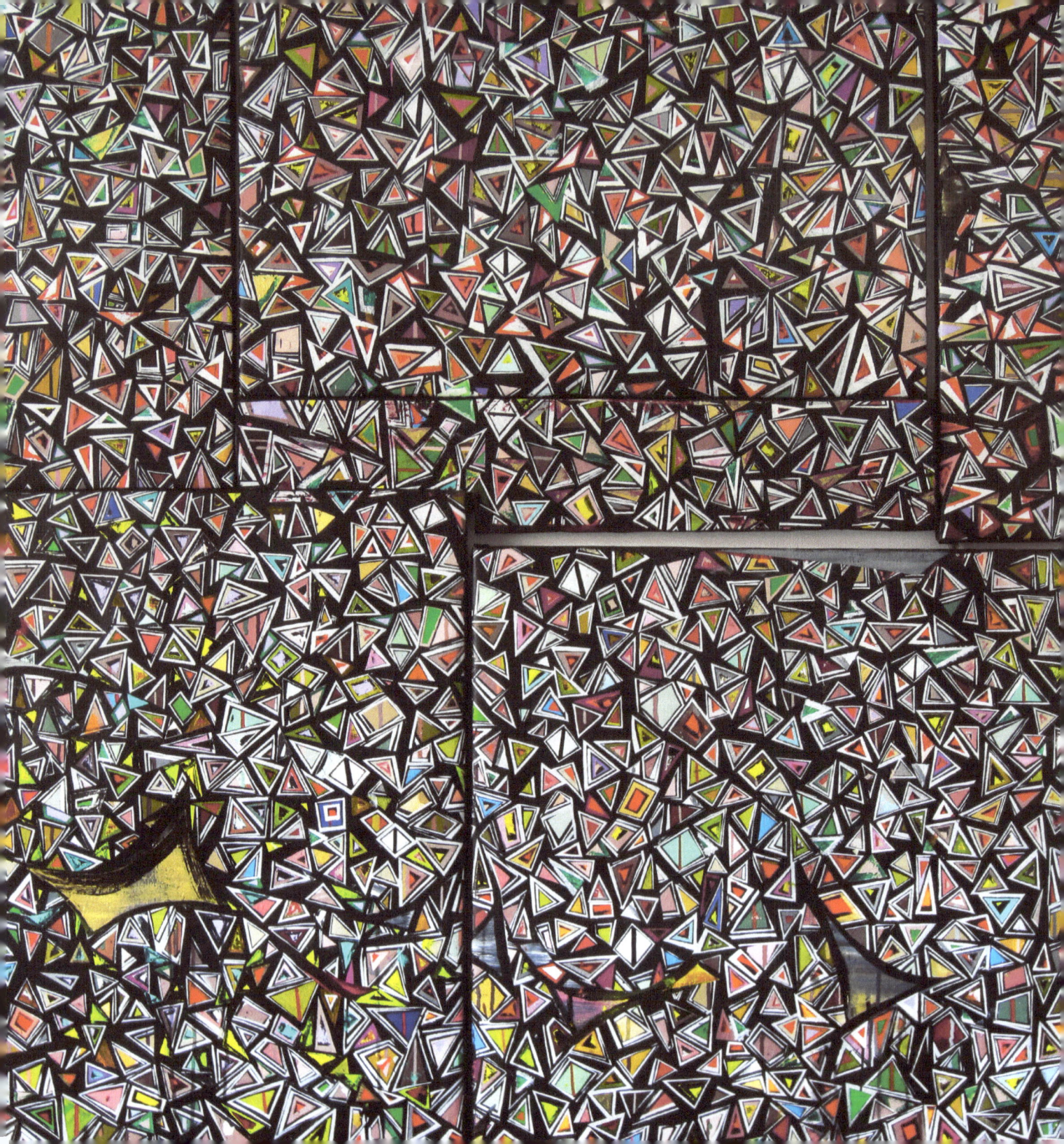

GREG BRICKEY is an artist, musician, and Jersey City Government, Office of Cultural Affairs Arts Curator for most of the last decade. He directs all art-related activities for Jersey City, working with Jersey City Redevelopment, the Mayor's office and as liaison to numerous community groups. He was previously President of Pro Arts Jersey City.

He is guitarist for his band One Hundred Hits.

Greg's work explores many aspects of drawing, abstract expressionism, graphic art, street art and graffiti. He builds chaotic, energetic structures out of independent graphic forms.

UNTITLED, 2014, ACRYLIC ON CANVAS, 72 IN. × 76 IN. DETAIL

UNTITLED, 2014, ACRYLIC ON CANVAS, 72 IN. × 76 IN.

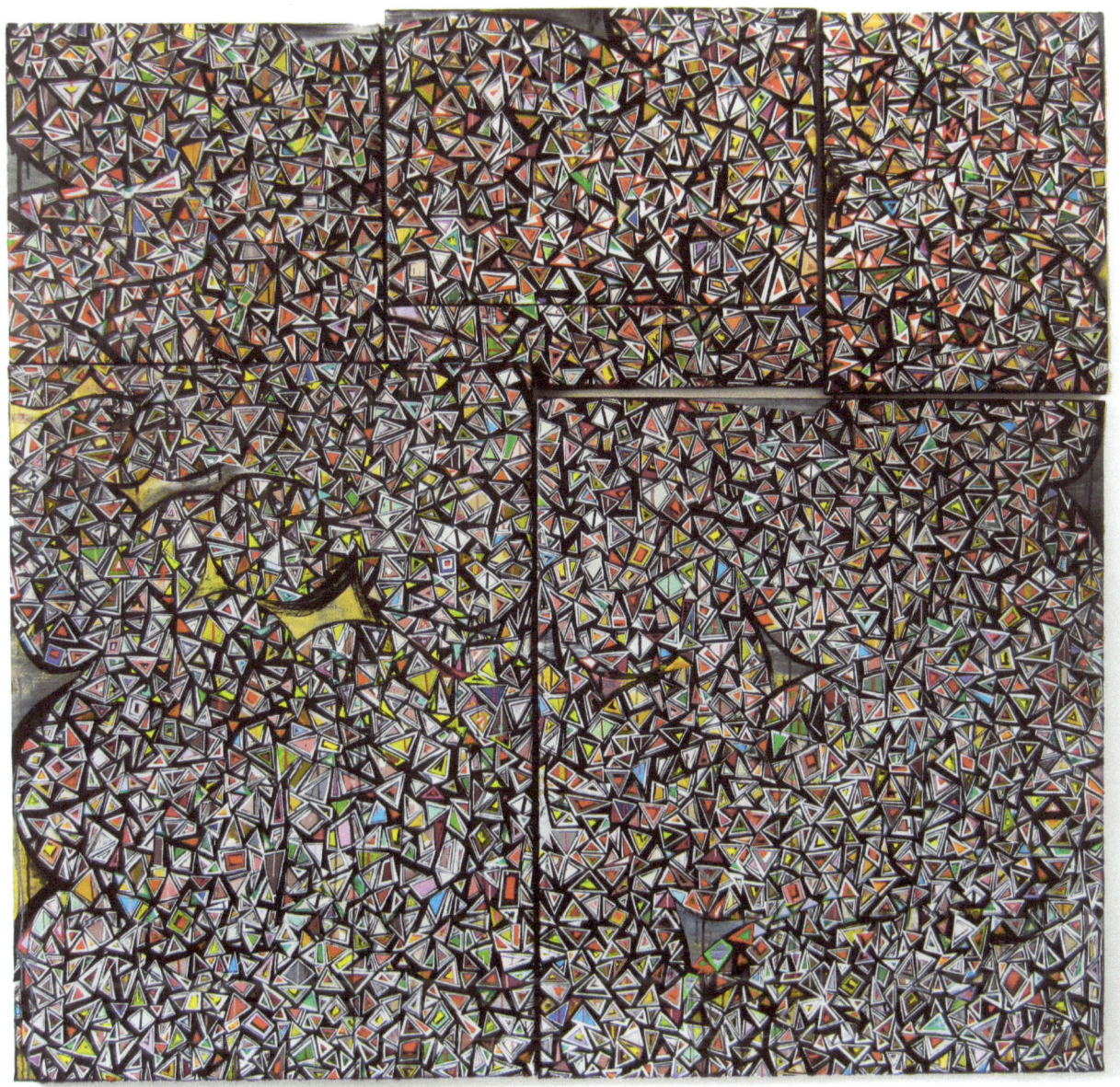

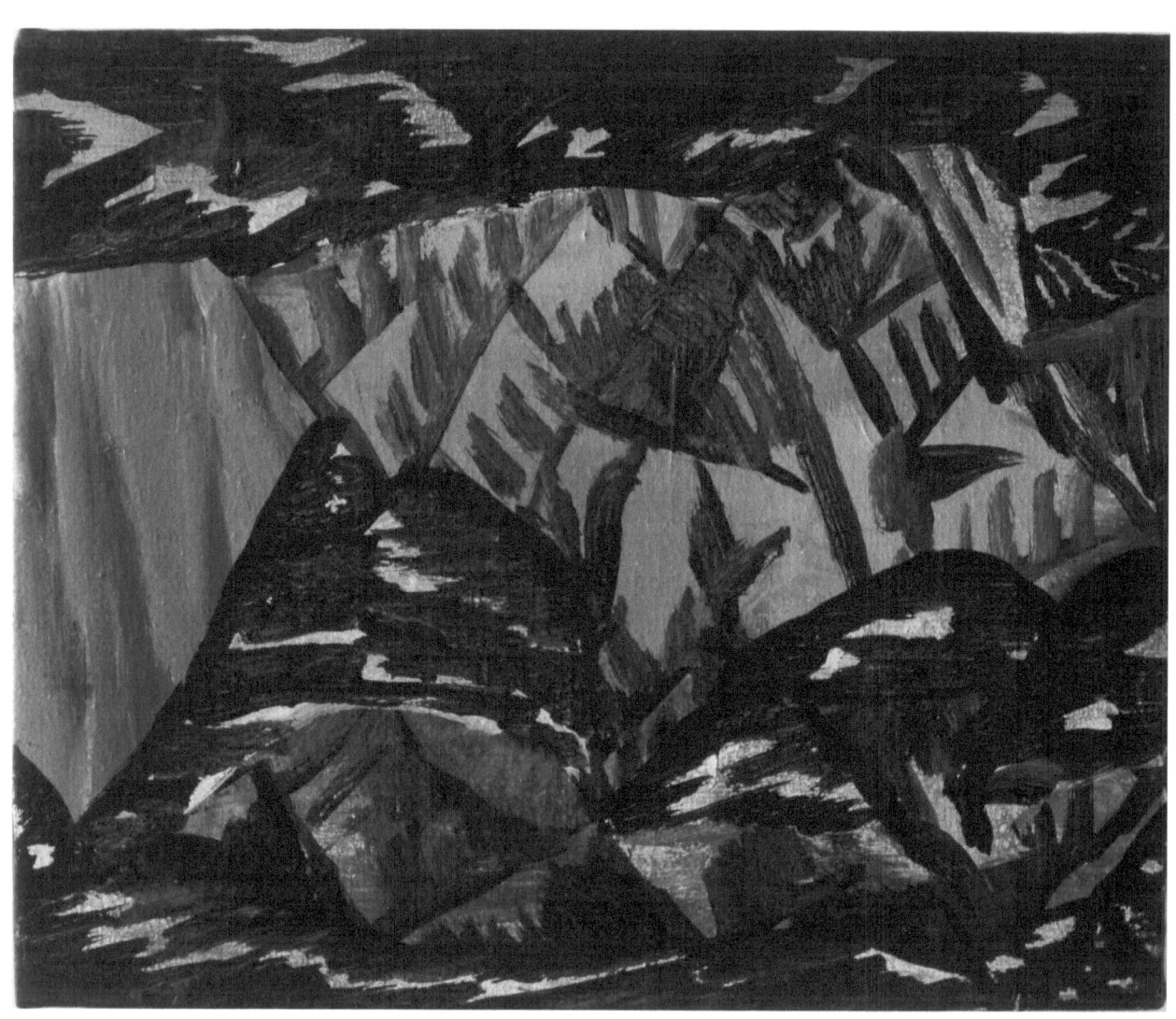

UNTITLED, 2014, INK ON PAPER, 12 IN. × 16 IN.

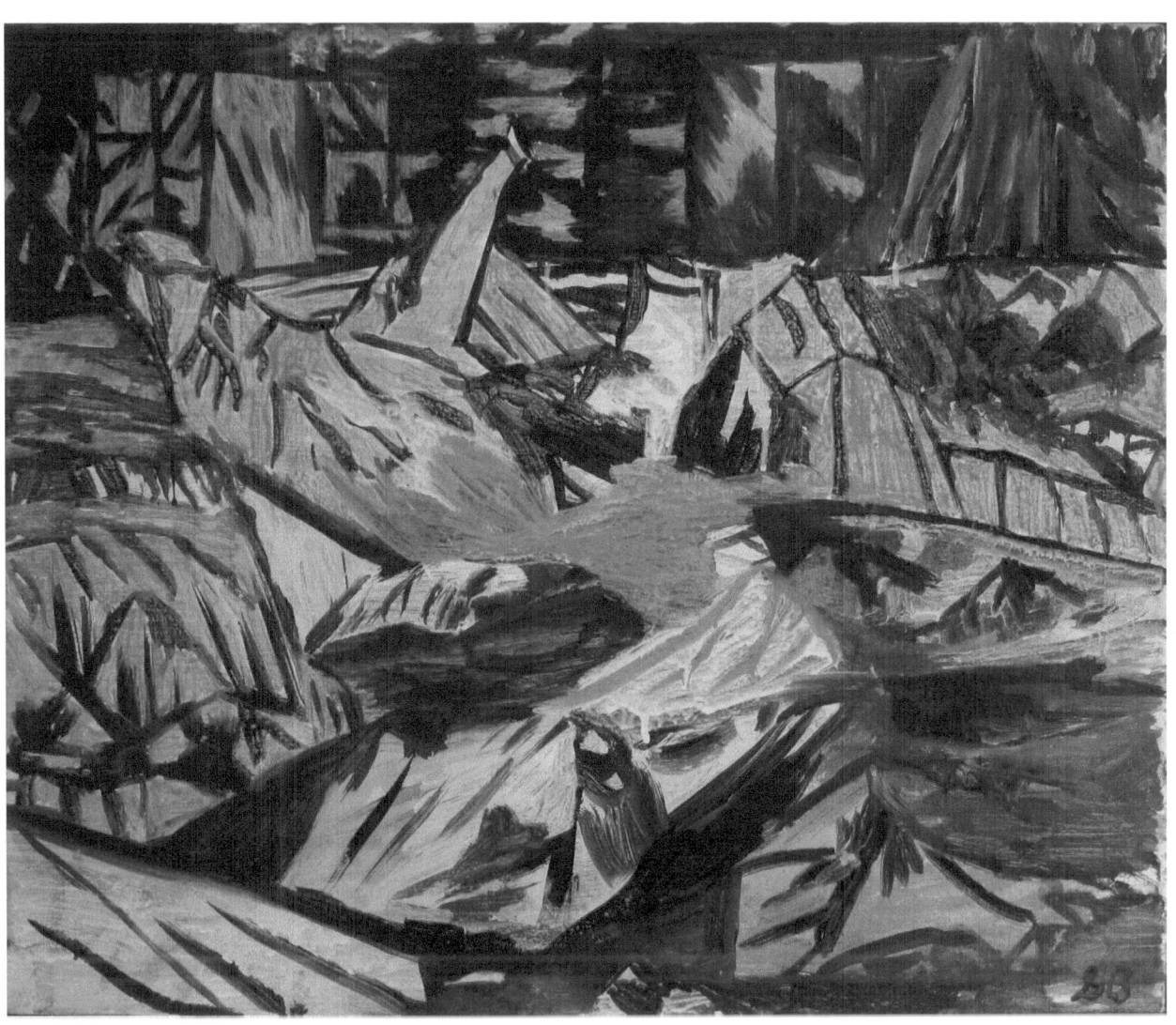

UNTITLED, 2014, INK ON PAPER, 21 IN. × 26 IN.

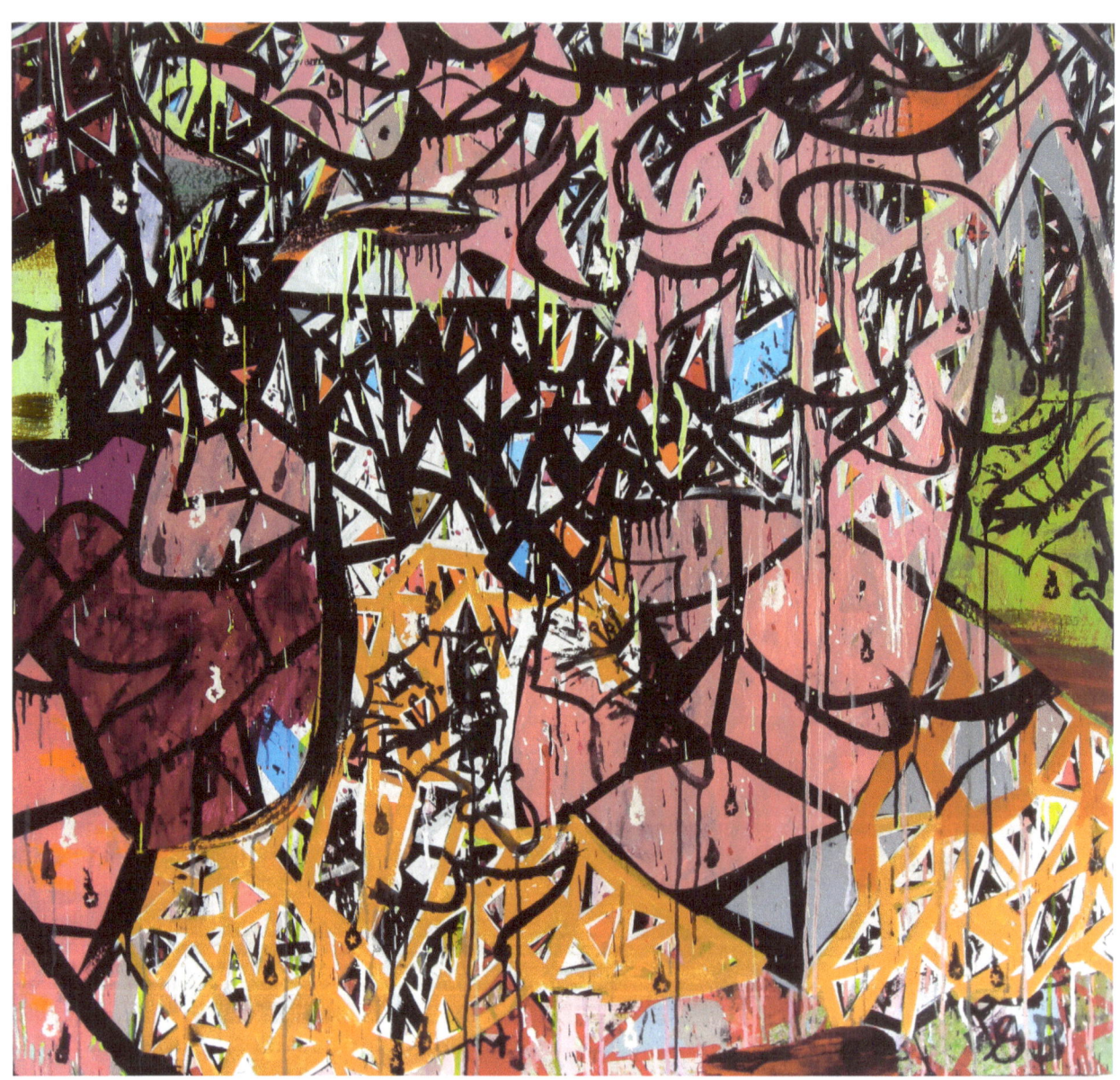

UNTITLED, 2014, ACRYLIC ON CANVAS, 44 IN. × 48 IN.

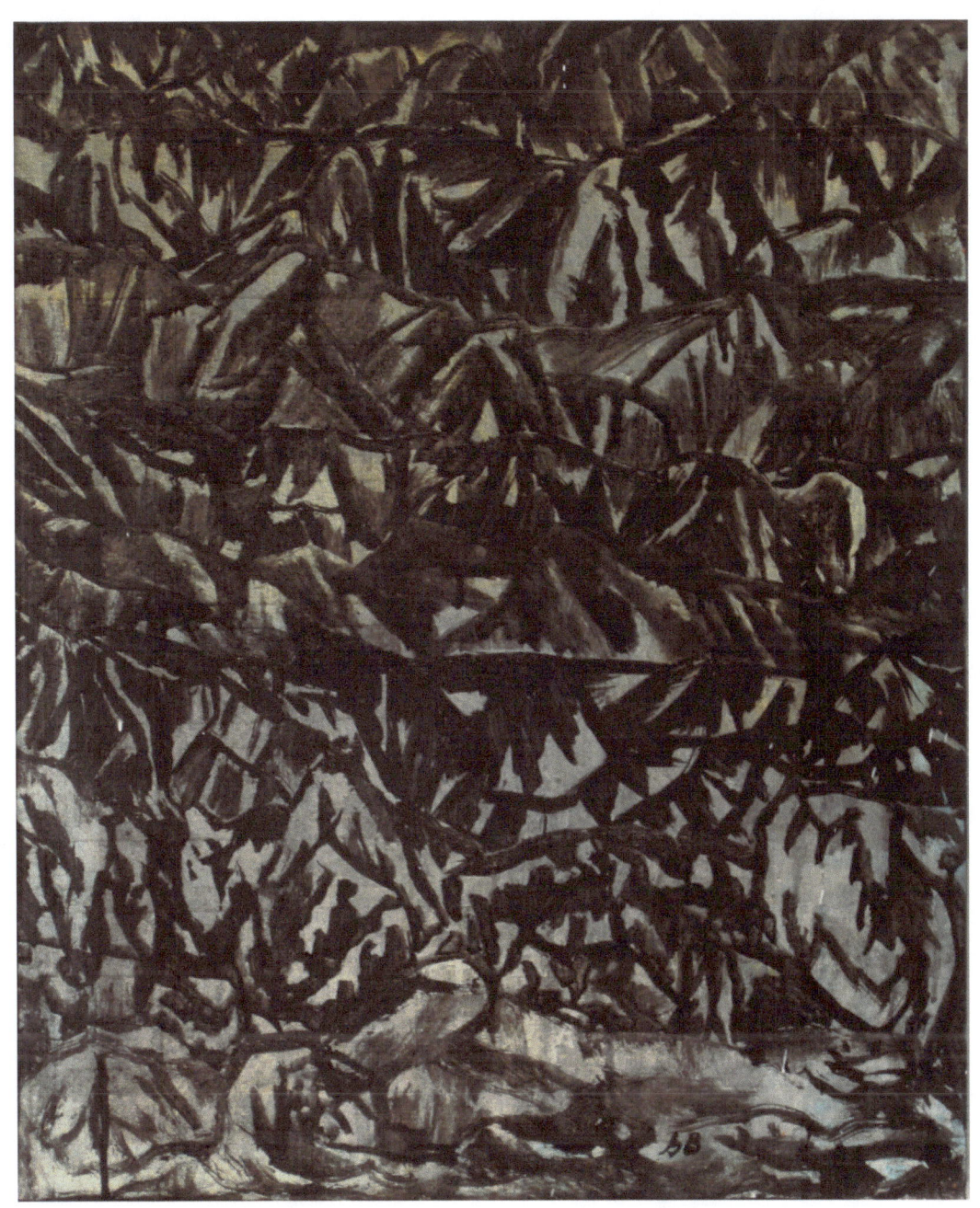

UNTITLED, 2014, INK ON CANVAS, 27 IN. × 16 IN.

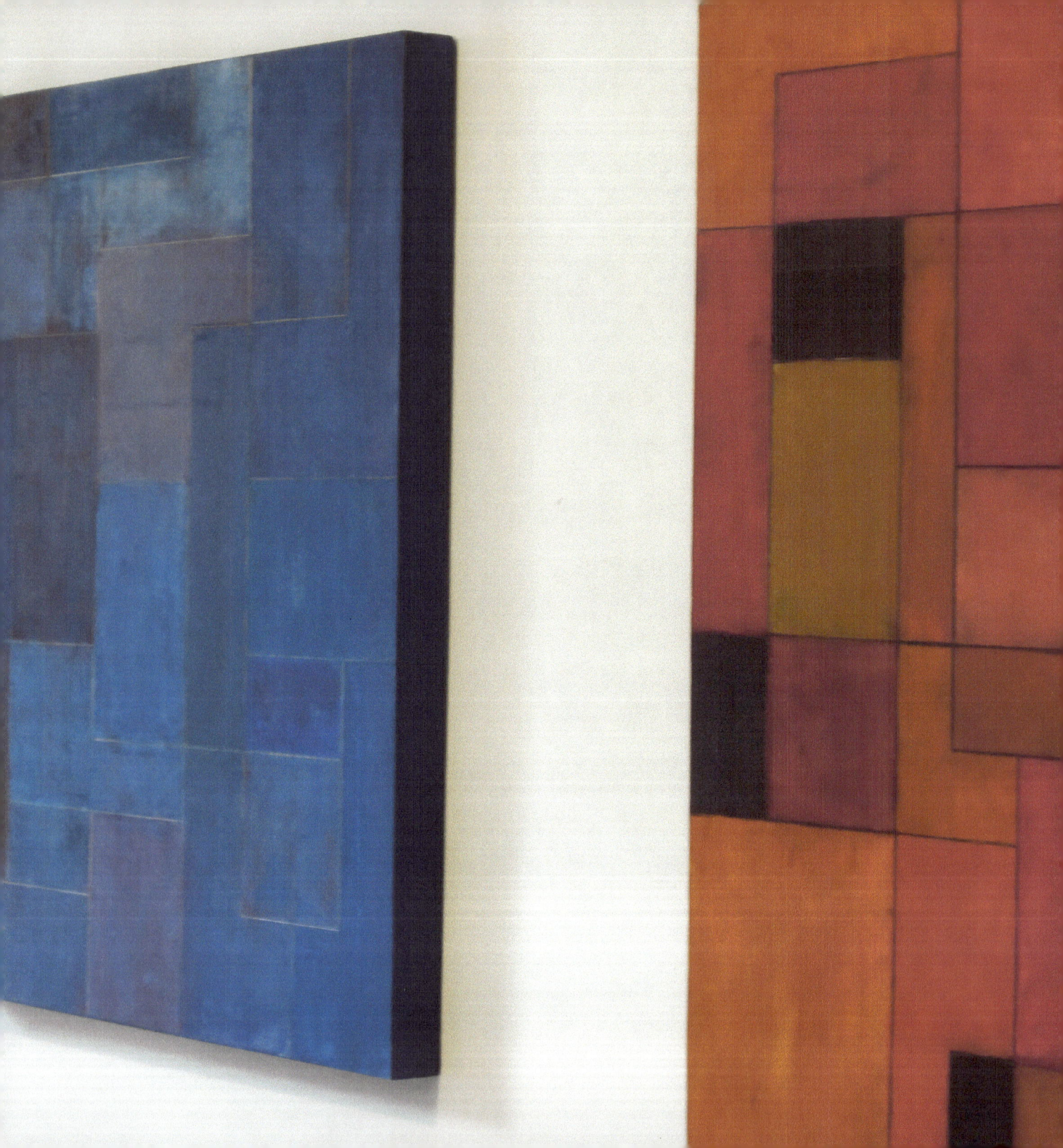

STEPHEN CIMINI *Building on the architectural origins which have been the basis of my work for over a decade, these new paintings on paper employ an emphasis on random symmetry allowing a pleasing, meditative composition to emerge.*

The impulsive color choices are fueled by intuition and experience.— SC

UNTITLED PAINTINGS, 2014, OIL PAINT AND WAX MEDIUM ON PAPER MOUNTED ON CRADLED WOOD PANEL
FINISHED WITH A PROTECTIVE WAX FINISH, 24 IN. × 20 IN.

UNTITLED, 2014, OIL PAINT AND WAX MEDIUM ON PAPER MOUNTED ON CRADLED WOOD PANEL FINISHED WITH A PROTECTIVE WAX FINISH, 10 IN. × 8 IN.

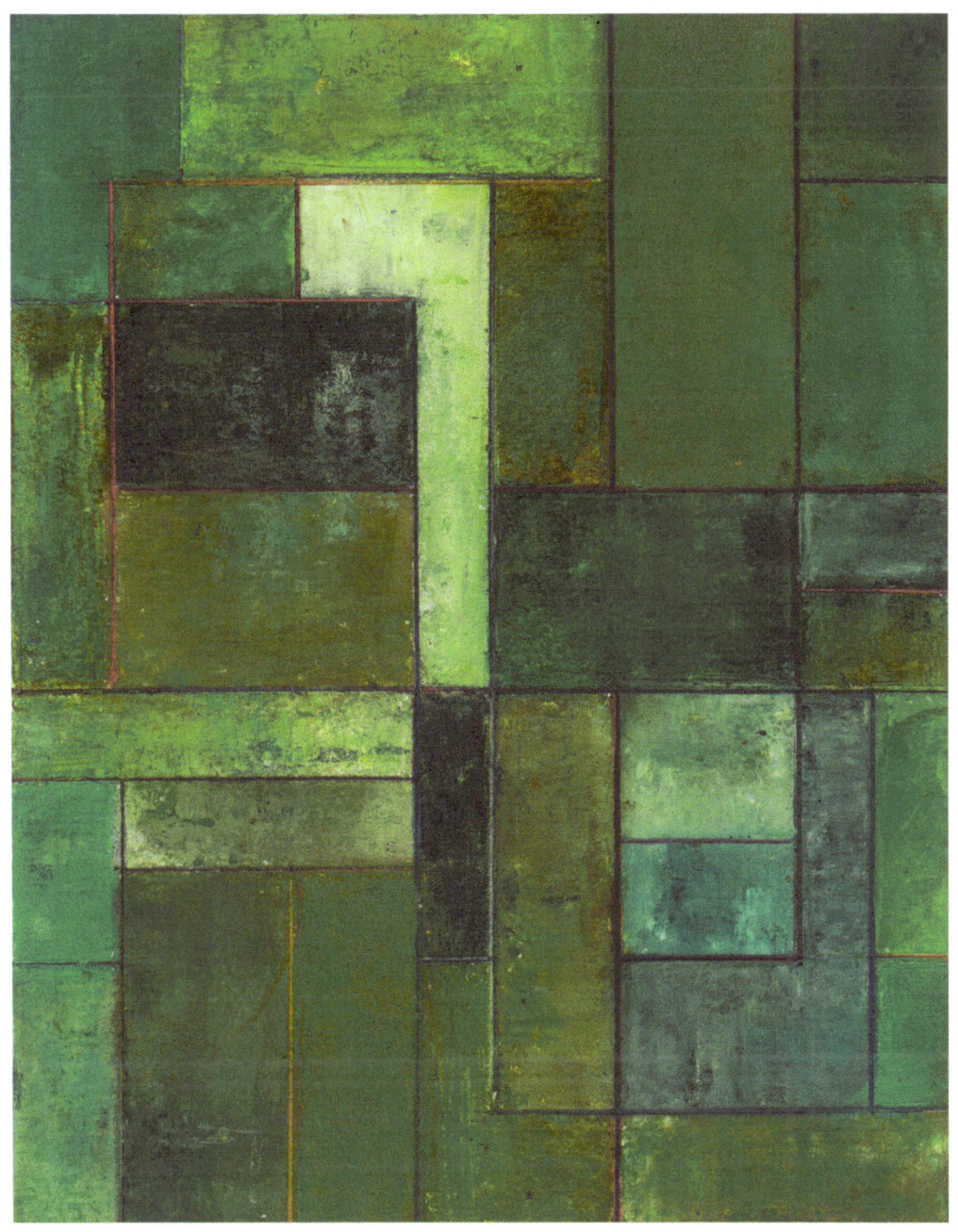

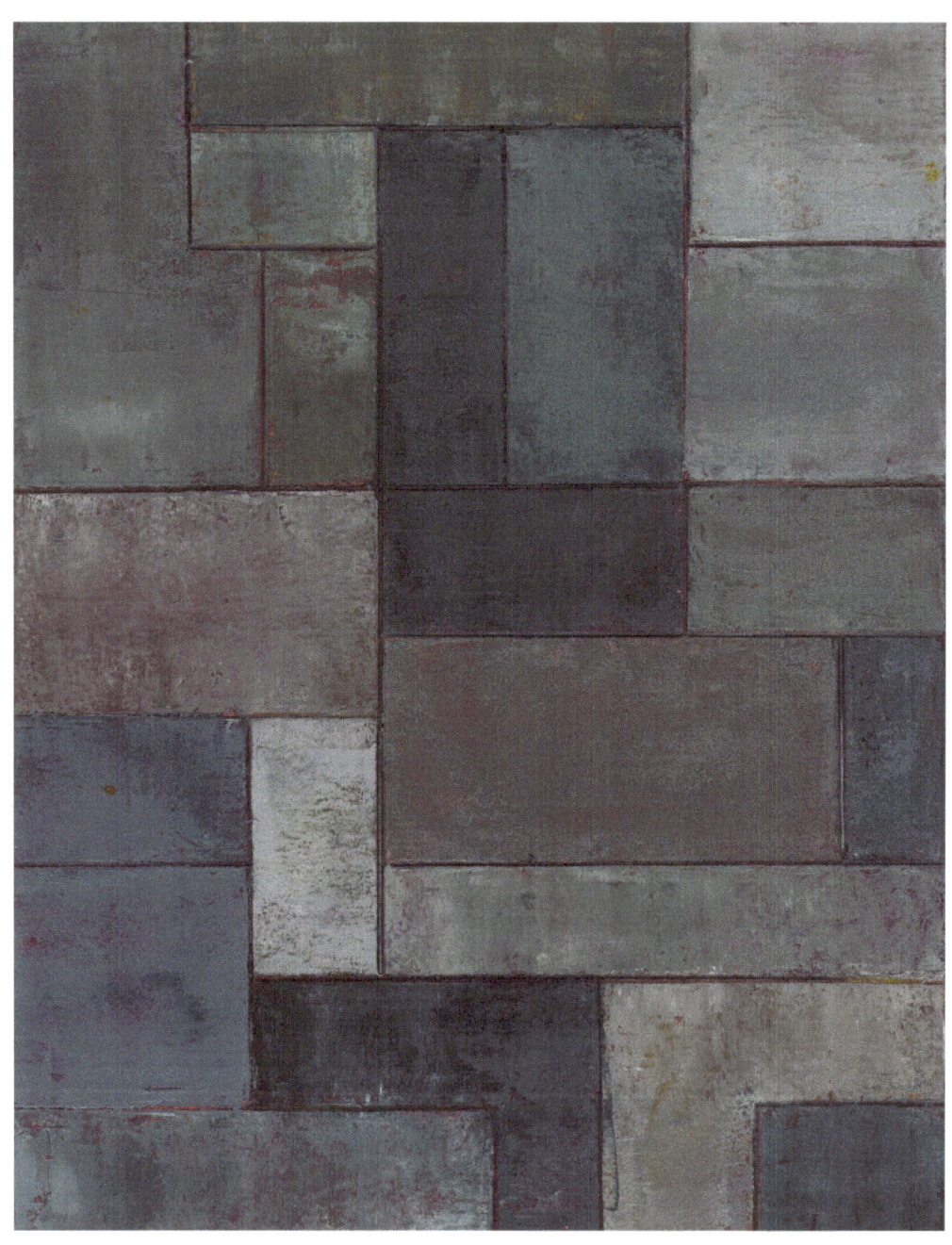

UNTITLED, 2014, OIL PAINT AND WAX MEDIUM ON PAPER MOUNTED ON CRADLED WOOD PANEL FINISHED WITH A PROTECTIVE WAX FINISH, 10 IN. × 8 IN.

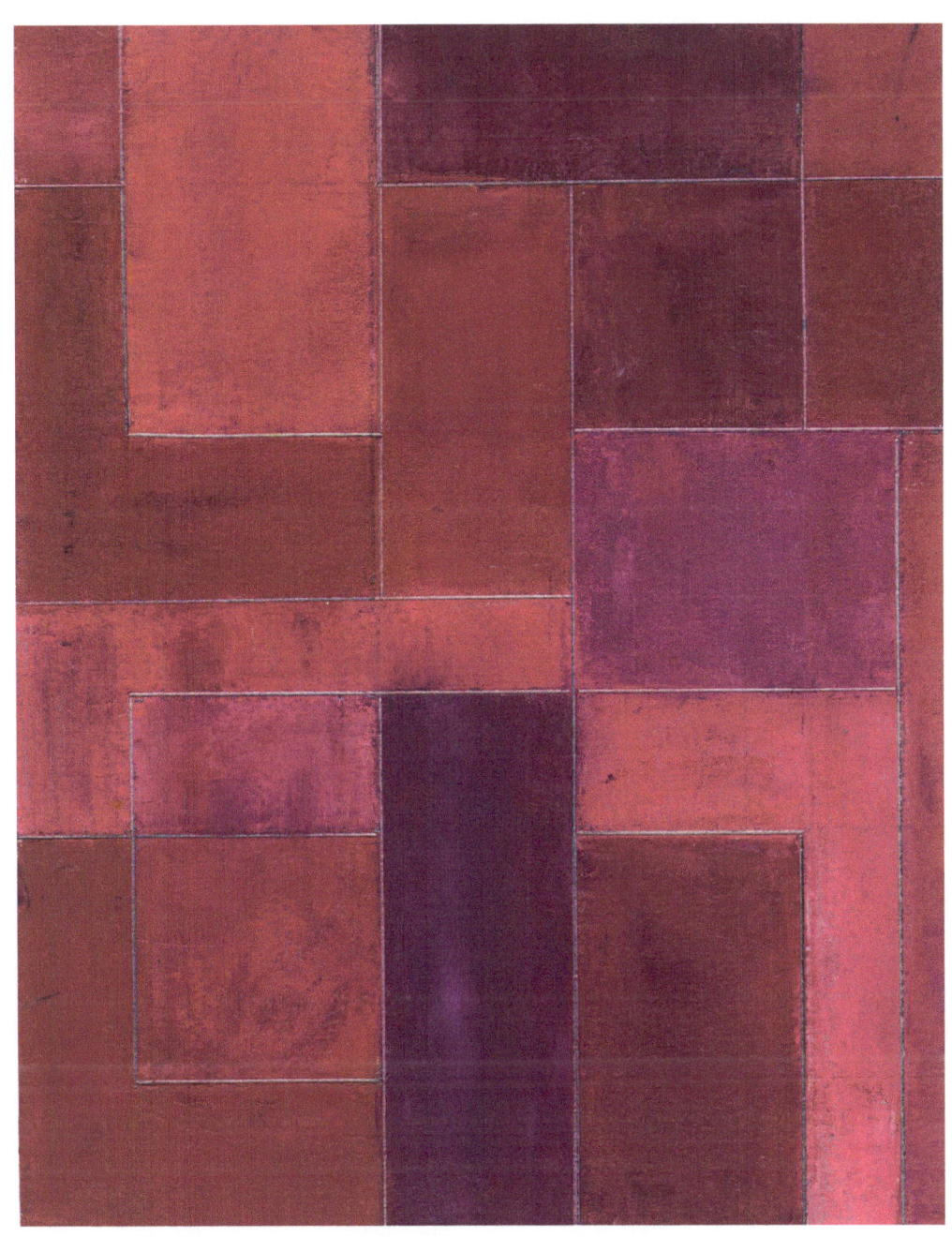

UNTITLED, 2014, OIL PAINT AND WAX MEDIUM ON PAPER MOUNTED ON CRADLED WOOD PANEL FINISHED WITH A PROTECTIVE WAX FINISH, 10 IN. × 8 IN.

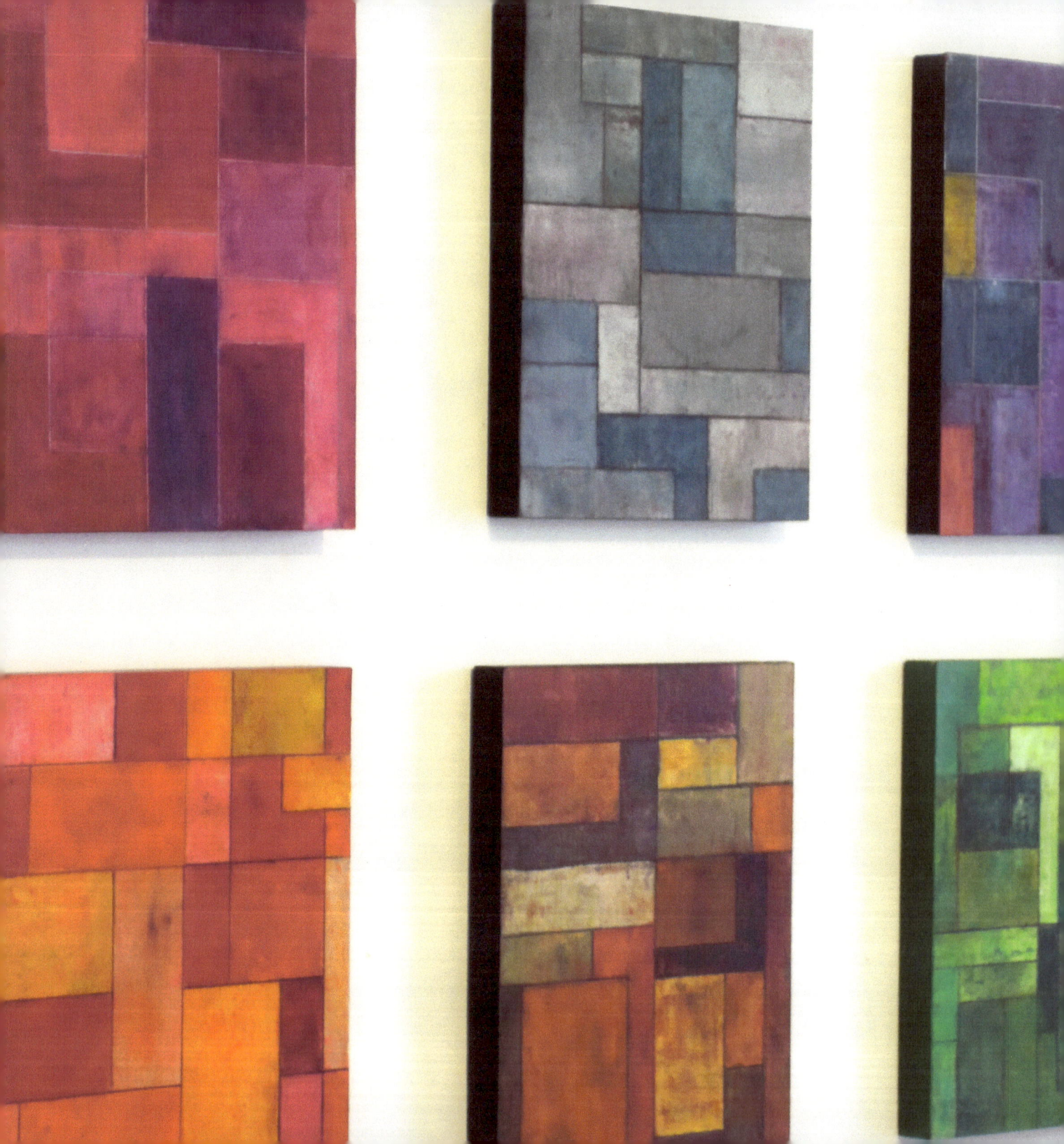

UNTITLED PAINTINGS, 2014, OIL PAINT AND WAX
MEDIUM ON PAPER MOUNTED ON CRADLED
WOOD PANEL FINISHED WITH A PROTECTIVE WAX
FINISH, 24 IN. × 20 IN.

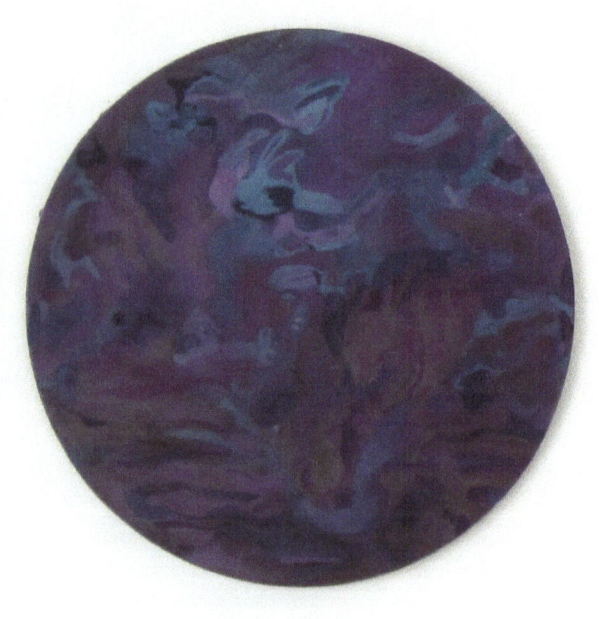
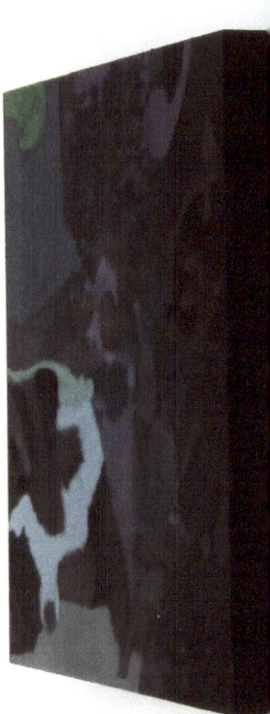

ROBYN ELLENBOGEN Childhood memories suggest that sensations captured my mind and spirit. I was drawn to the darkness of the night sky, the smoothness of surfaces, and the play of light and pattern that appeared when I closed my eyes. Time and memory play an important role in my work. I aspire to translate these feelings, perceptions, and sensations into something palpable, fluid , intimating the process by which formlessness becomes form. I work in varied formats, drawings, paintings, books, digital imagery, photography and sculpture, all based in an abstract language. Over the past few years I have been working in metalpoint and egg tempera. Both of these practices are based in 12th century techniques. Metalpoint was used in several ways, drawing, preliminary sketch for painting (often egg tempera) and calligraphy. My work challenges traditional concepts of representation. I use an assortment of metalpoint and metallic wools. Metalpoint may include metal wire in a stylus and the use of flat and three-dimensional pieces of metal such as coins, plates spoons and assorted jewelry. I draw with everyday objects and build dream-like images in which fiction and reality meet, meanings shift and past and present fuse. Who can say what memory is? My images occur from intuitive and internal gestures, These gestures generate seemingly tranquil images that leave traces on the edge of recognition and alienation. My paintings in egg tempera continue to explore inner states of mind. When I was a child, my internal dialogue often centered on loss, absence, the inevitability of dying and a sense of absurdity. Egg tempera paintings are often combined with the use of metalpoint. I rarely work from a sketch or a plan but more often a generalized feeling, thought, or emotion. Making art allows me to grasp the world as a paradoxical break with familiar acceptance.

[LEFT] *ABUNDANCE*, 2013, EGG TEMPERA, METALLIC WOOL, METALPOINT, COLORED GESSO ON MAPLE, 10 IN. DIAMETER

[RIGHT] *BORN UNDER A BAD SIGN*, 2013, EGG TEMPERA, METALPOINT, COLORED GESSO ON PANEL, 10 IN. × 10 IN.

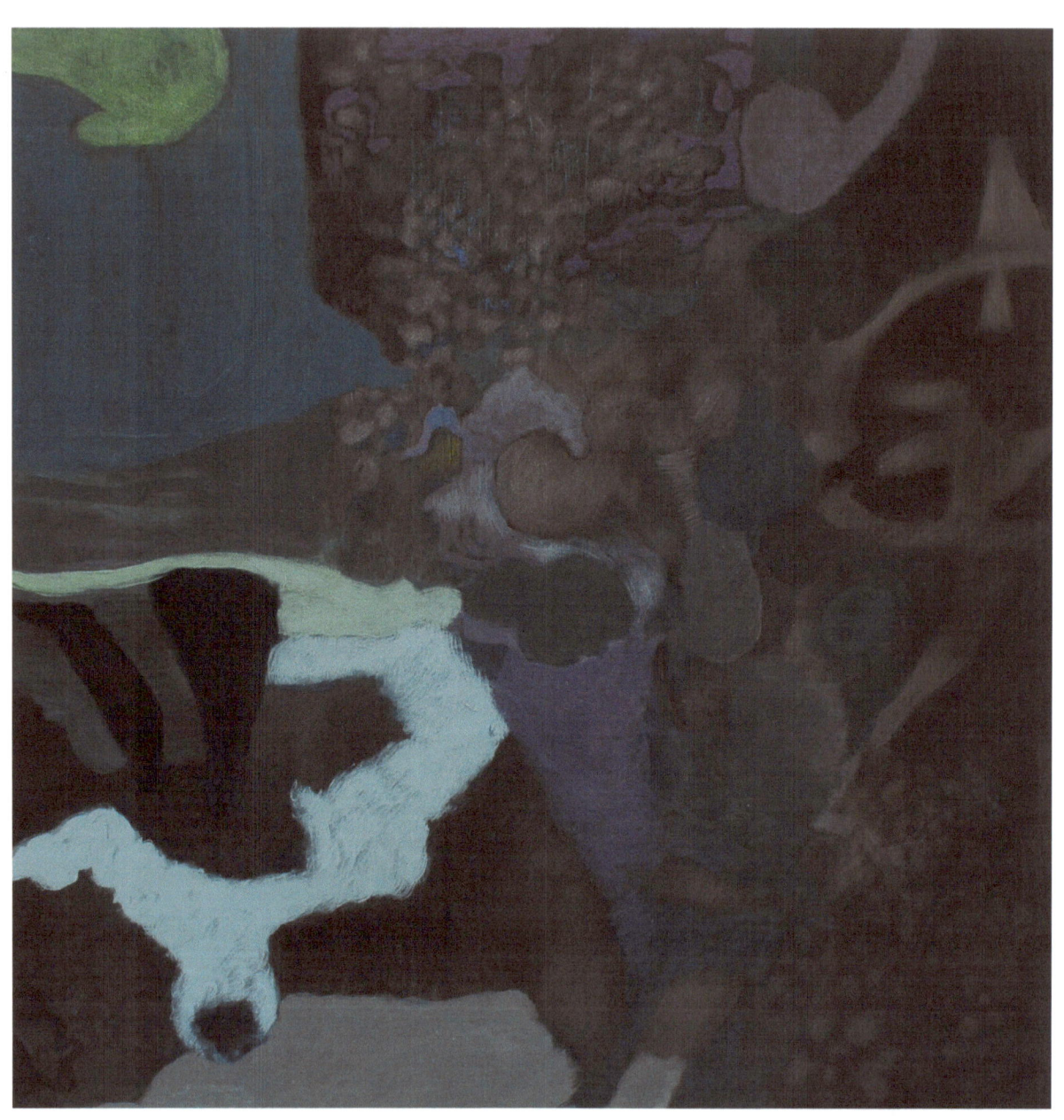

BORN UNDER A BAD SIGN, 2013, EGG TEMPERA, METALPOINT, COLORED GESSO ON PANEL, 10 IN. × 10 IN.

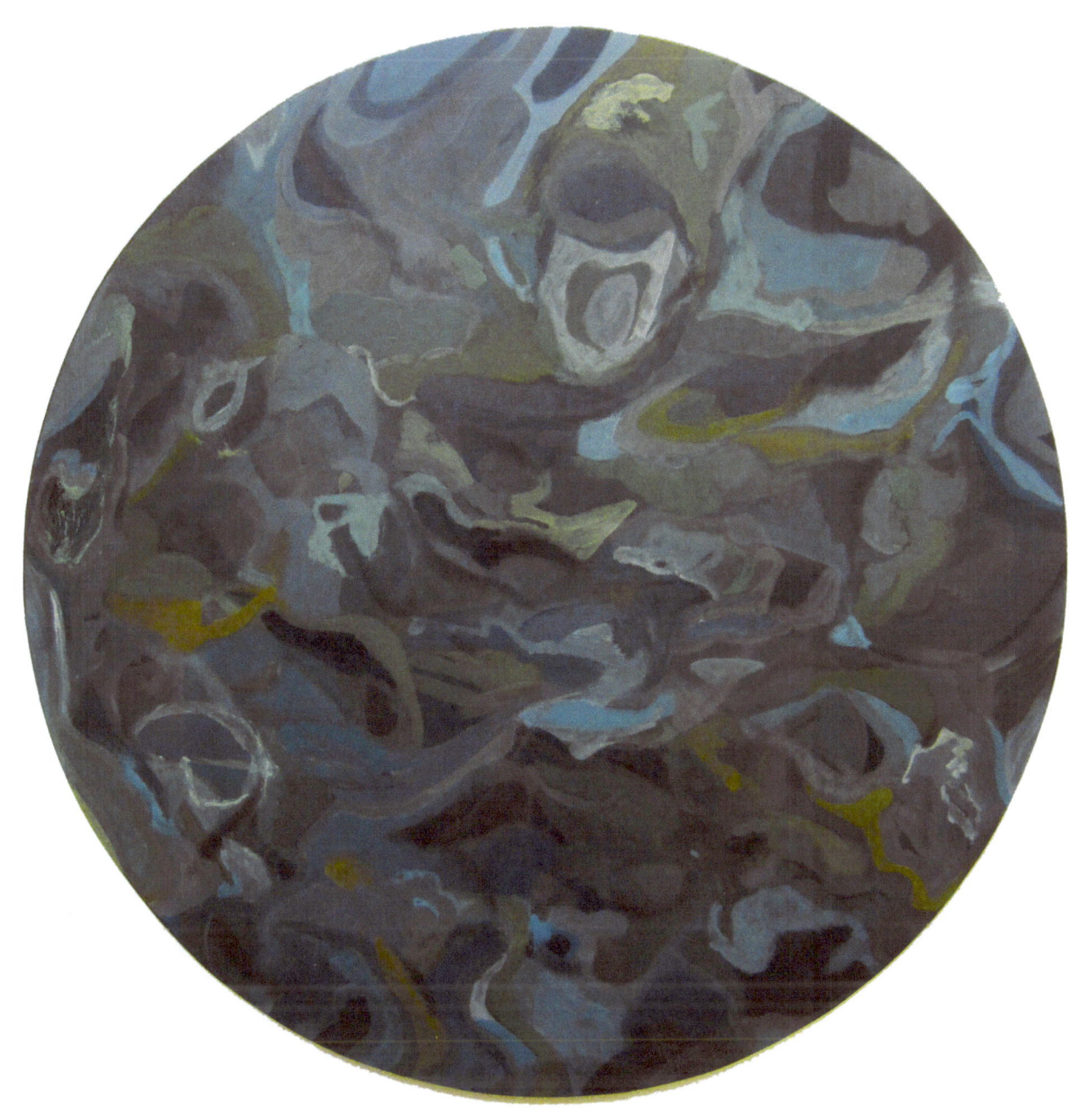

OW OUT OF THE NOW, 2013, EGG TEMPERA, METALLIC WOOL, METALPOINT, COLORED GESSO ON MAPLE, 12 IN. DIAMETER

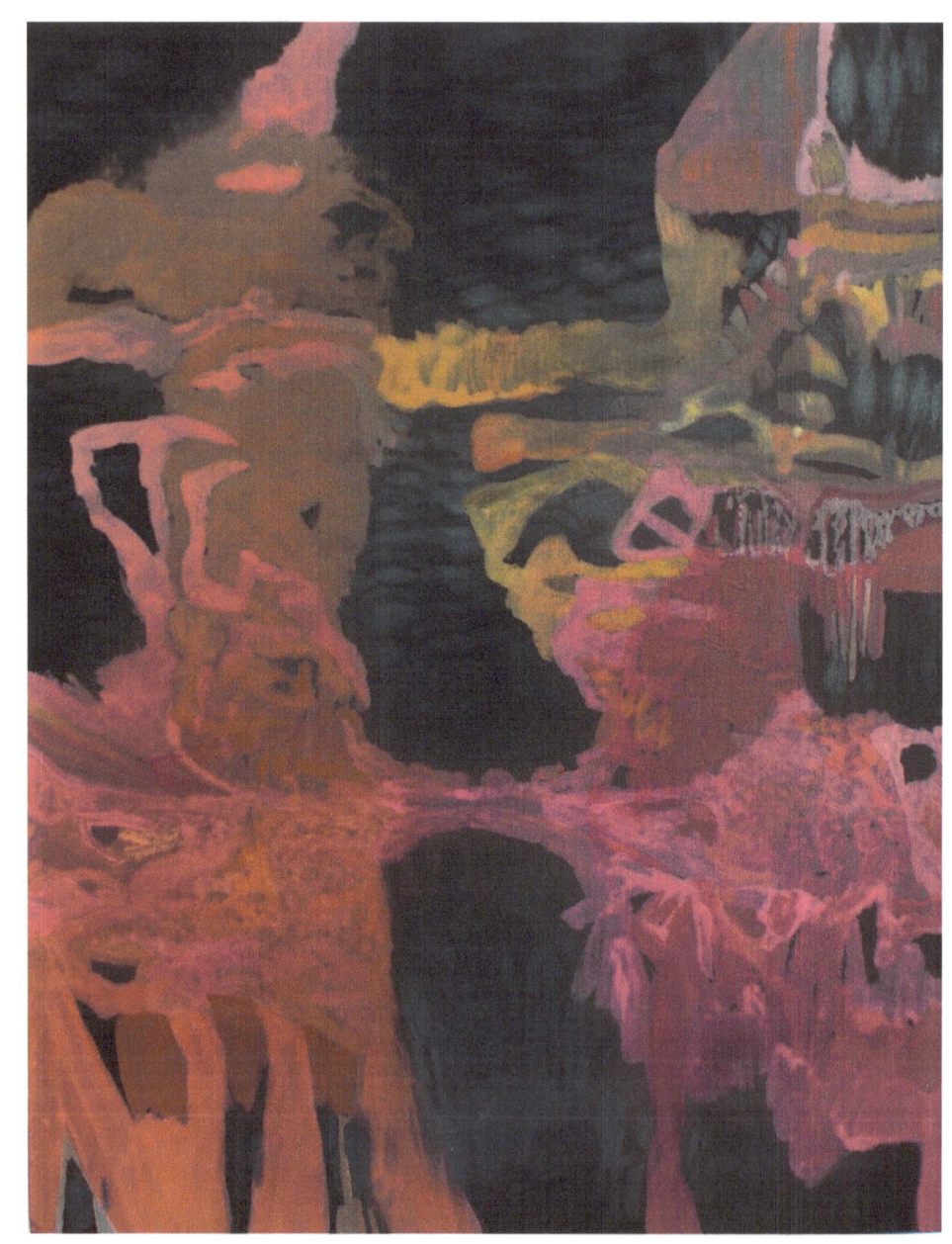

APPEARING-VANISHING, 2013, EGG TEMPERA, METALPOINT, COLORED GESSO ON PANEL, 10 IN. × 8 IN.

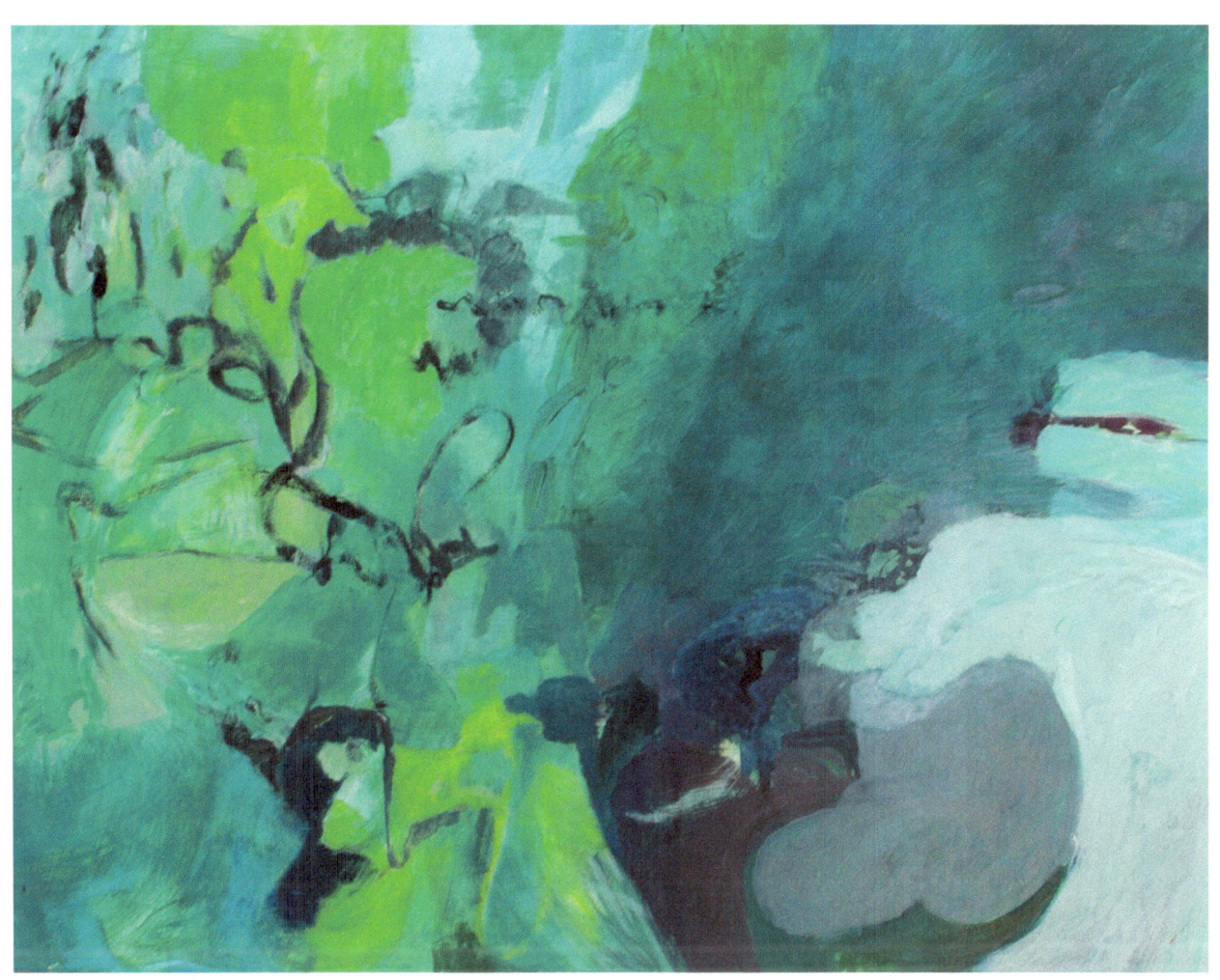

NEITHER INNER NOR OUTER, 2013, EGG TEMPERA ON PANEL, 16 IN. × 20 IN.

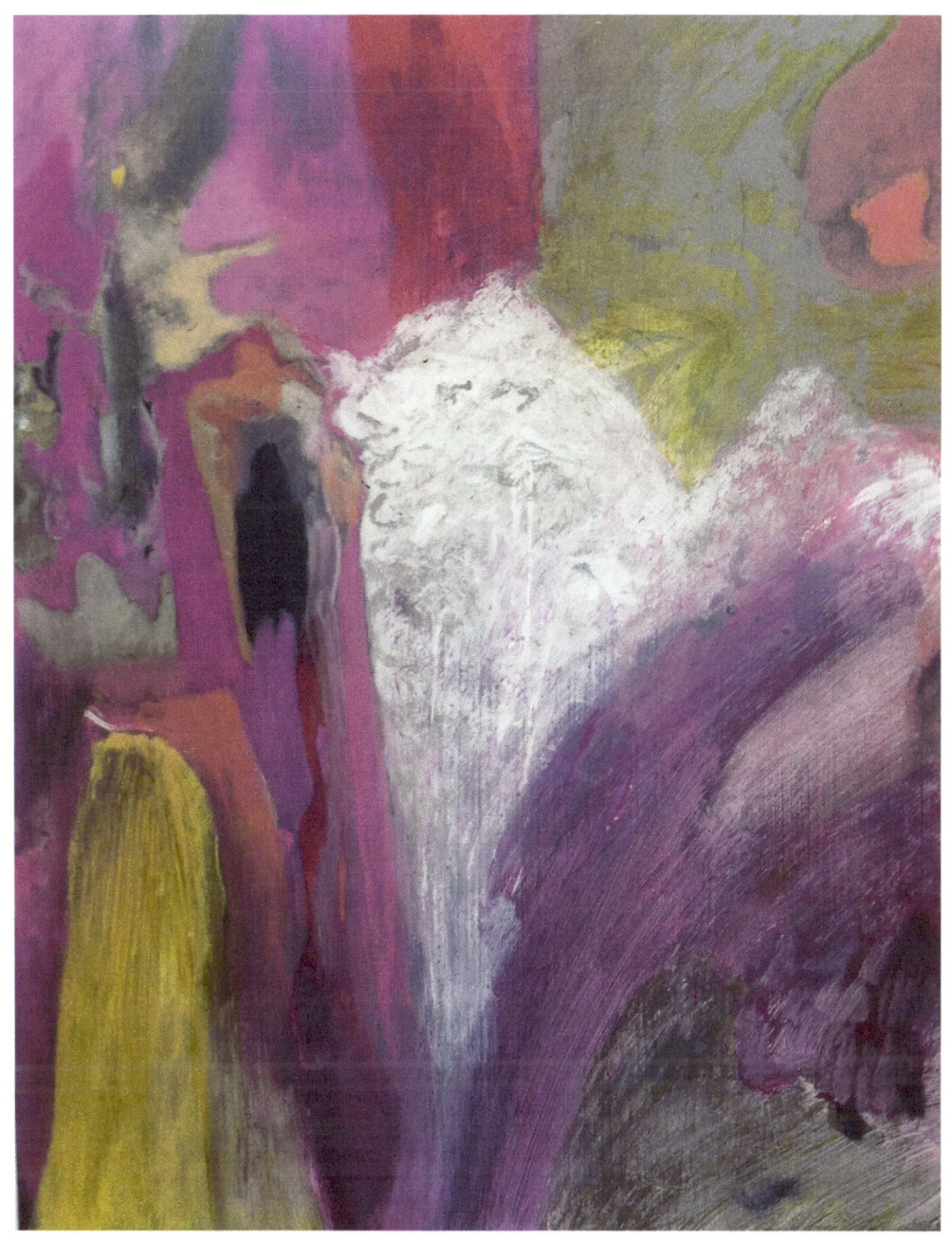

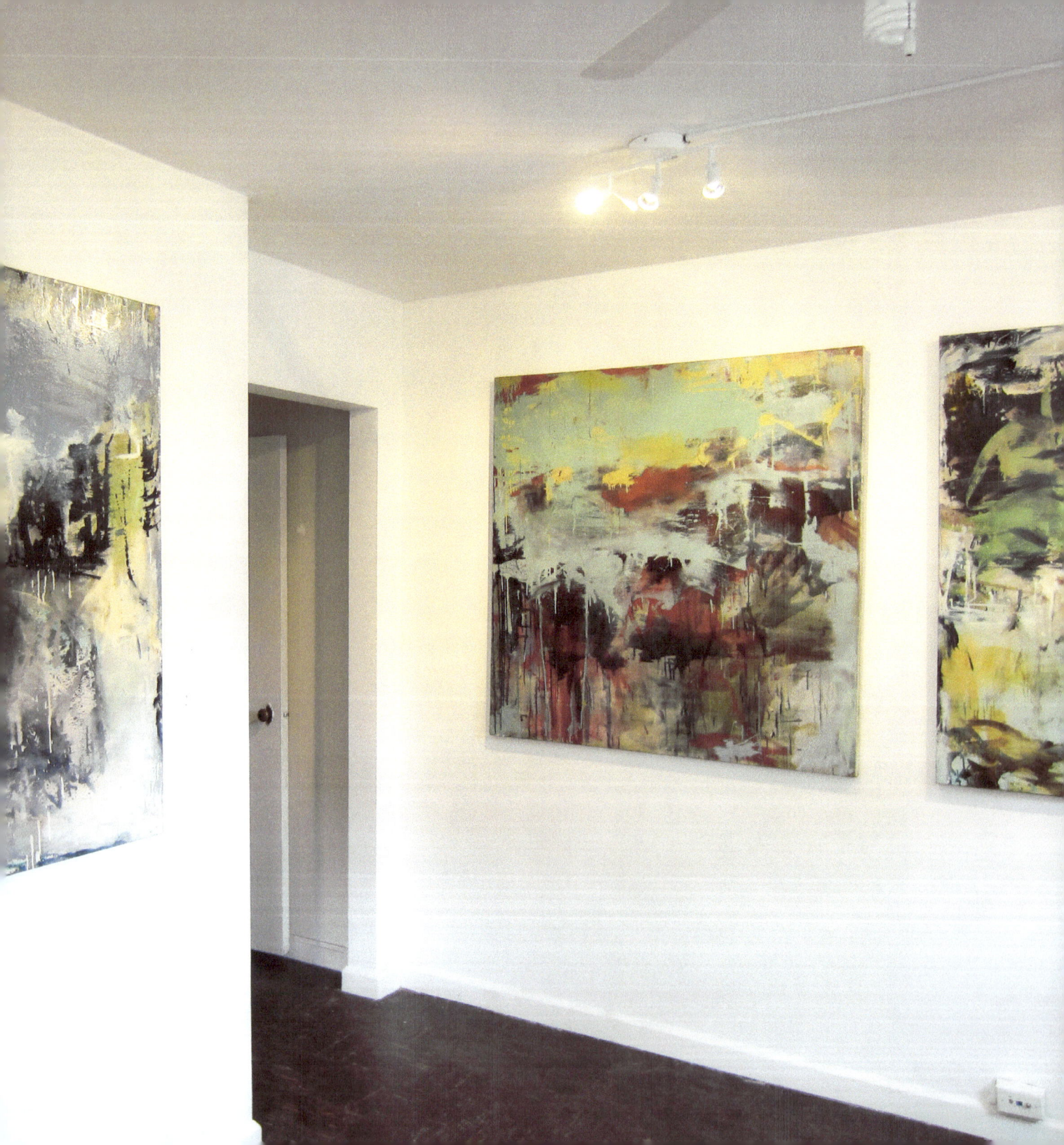

ROBIN FELD   "As an abstract painter I am interested in what happens in the world of a painting when serenity is invaded by a chaotic jumble of randomness.

There is a moment, or a series of moments that are pivotal in the creation of a painting… perhaps the same can be said, in the creation or living of a life. To differing degrees, we go along in our grids, in our bands of color, but inevitably, the unexpected happens and there is nothing to be done but cope as best we can.

In that spirit I am pouring, scraping and blotting paint, creating a kind of managed chaos. After the rush of adrenaline subsides, it is then my job to meditate on the results and work with them until the painting feels "right." I want the marks on the canvas to talk to each other, for the layers to interact, for the process of how the painting was built to be apparent.

Abstract expressionism, minimalism, Japanese and Chinese landscape painting and calligraphy are strong influences on my painting as are the grids and jumbles of Manhattan and Brooklyn and the line, shape, color and form that I "collect" while working with watercolor outdoors. I love the controlled randomness that drips create. The painting is built in layers using poured, scraped and brushed paints.

CRYSTALLIZED, 2013, OIL ON CANVAS, 44 IN. × 48 IN.

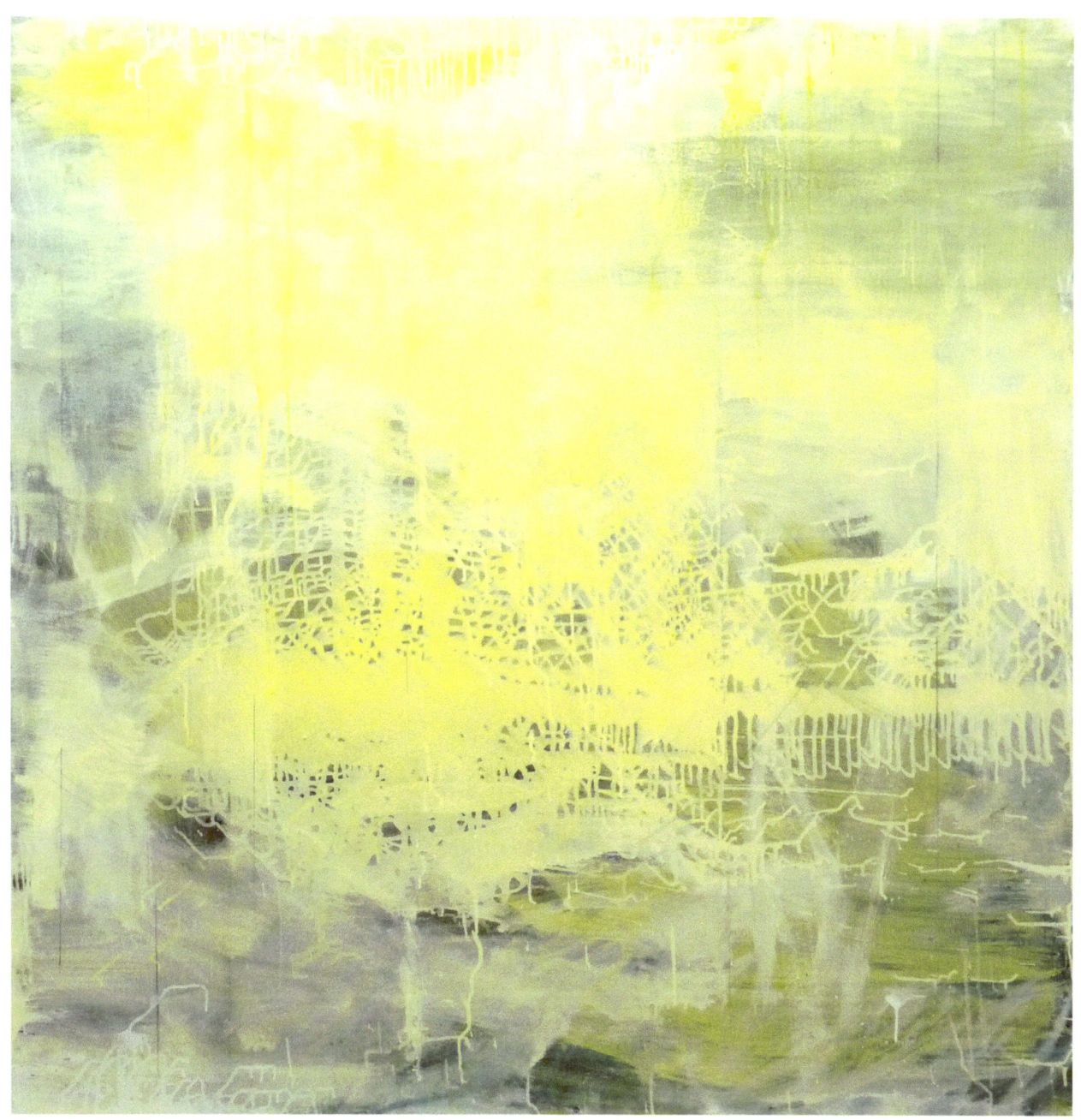

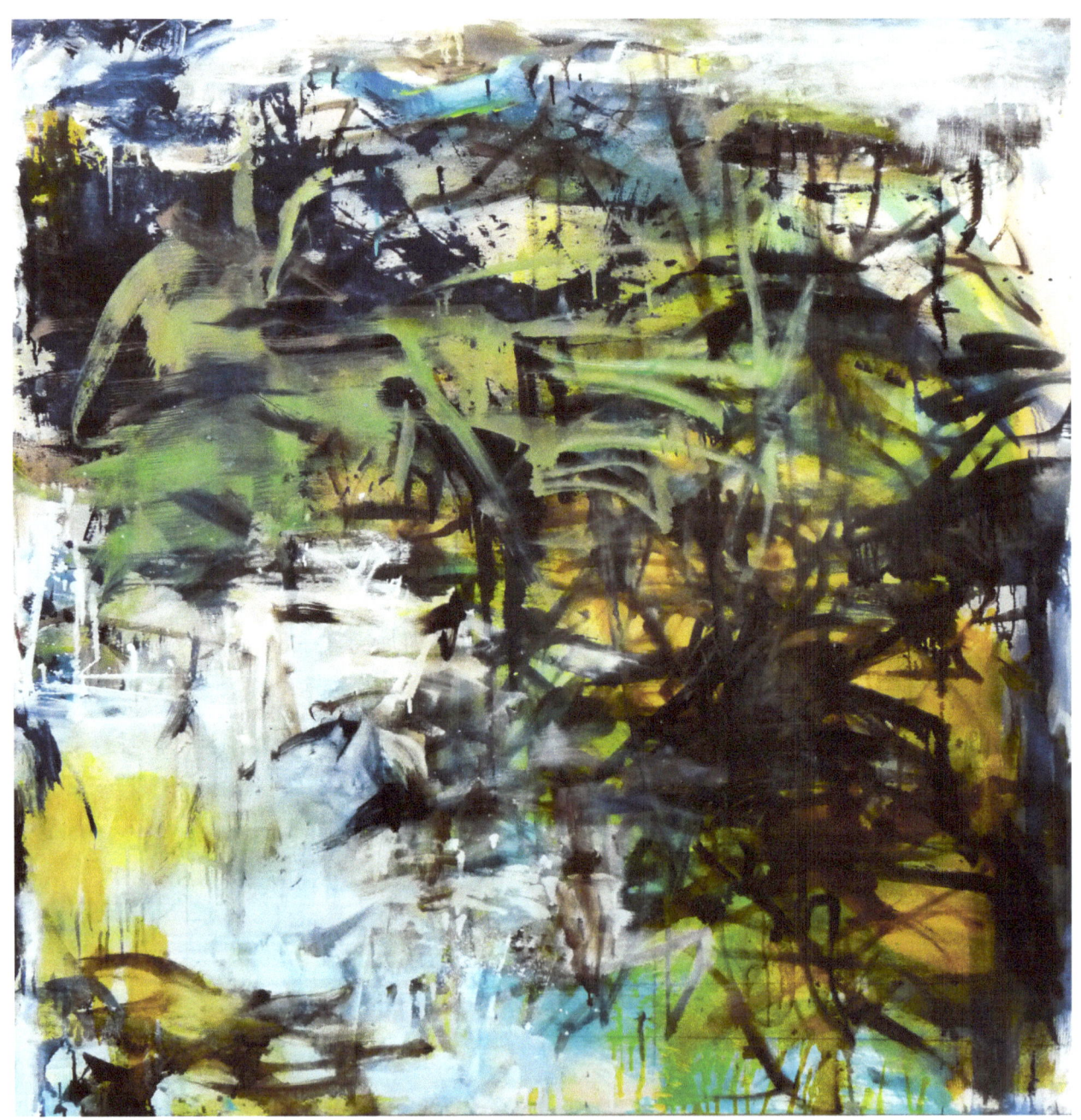

CYCLONE 2, 2013, OIL ON CANVAS, 44 IN. × 48 IN.

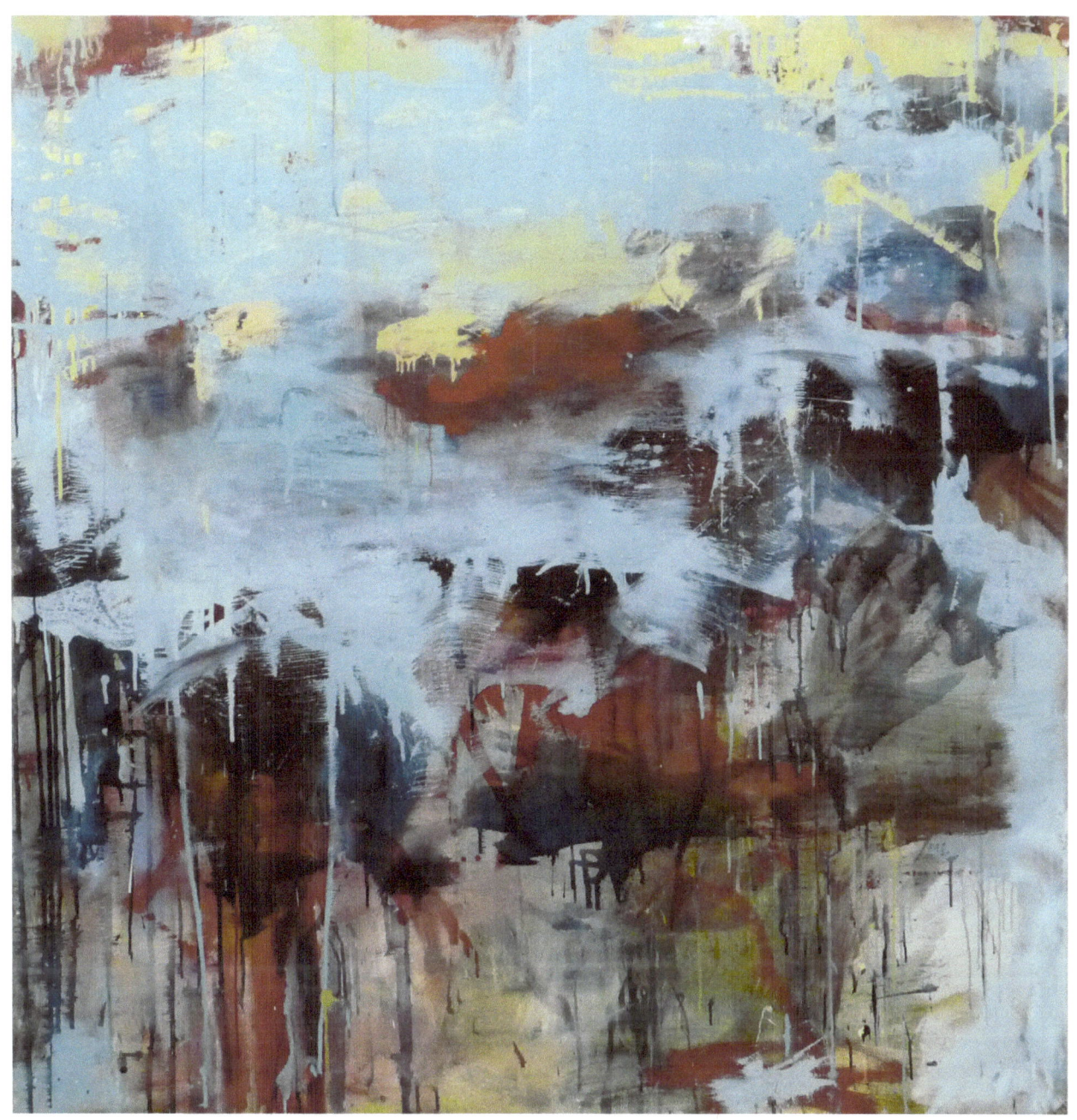

MORAL COMBAT, 2013, OIL ON CANVAS, 44 IN. x 48 IN.

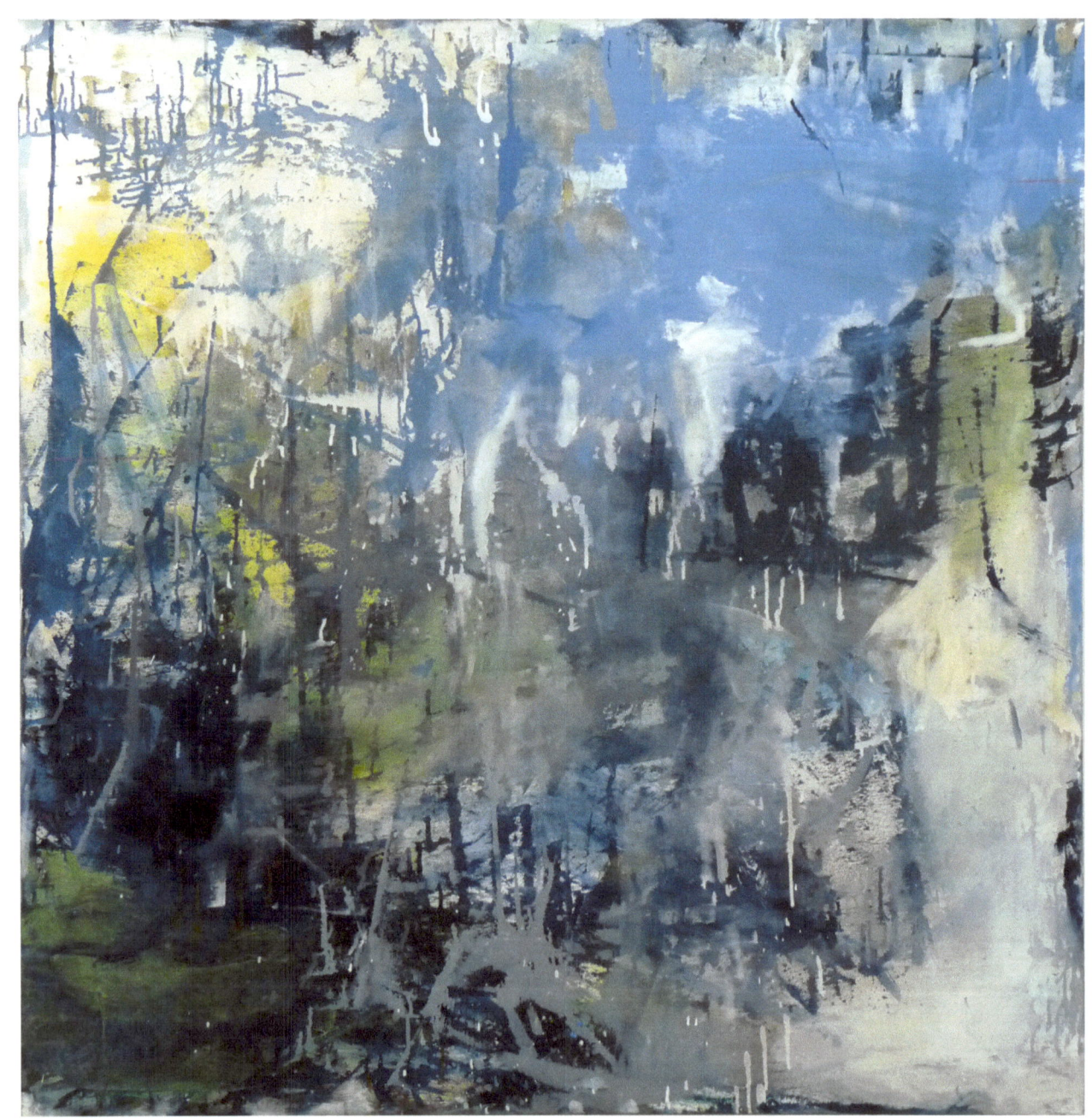

ALMOST REMEMBERED, 2013, OIL ON CANVAS, 44 IN. × 48 IN.

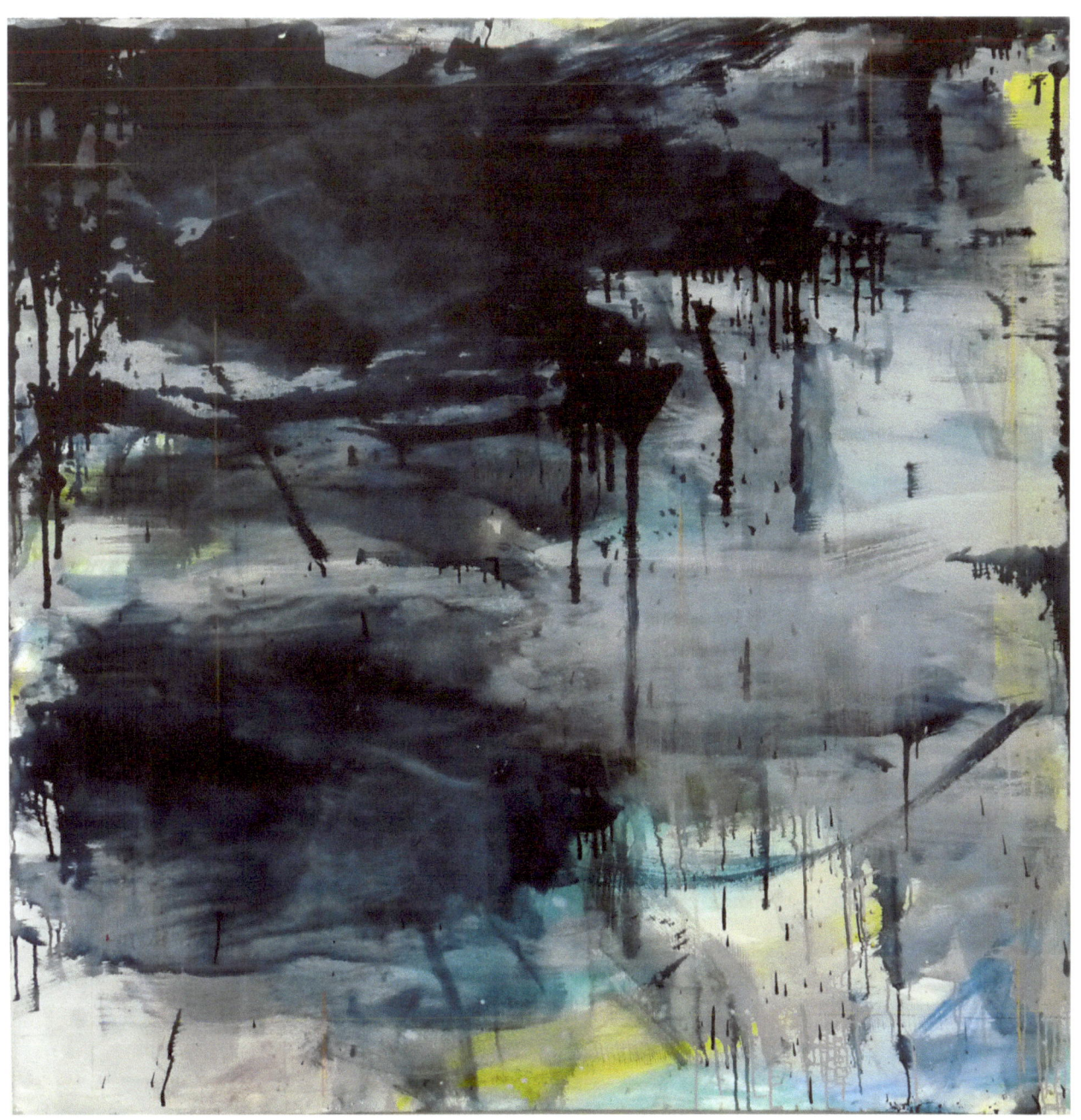

LOOMIN'BLUEZ, 2013, OIL ON CANVAS, 44 IN. × 48 IN.

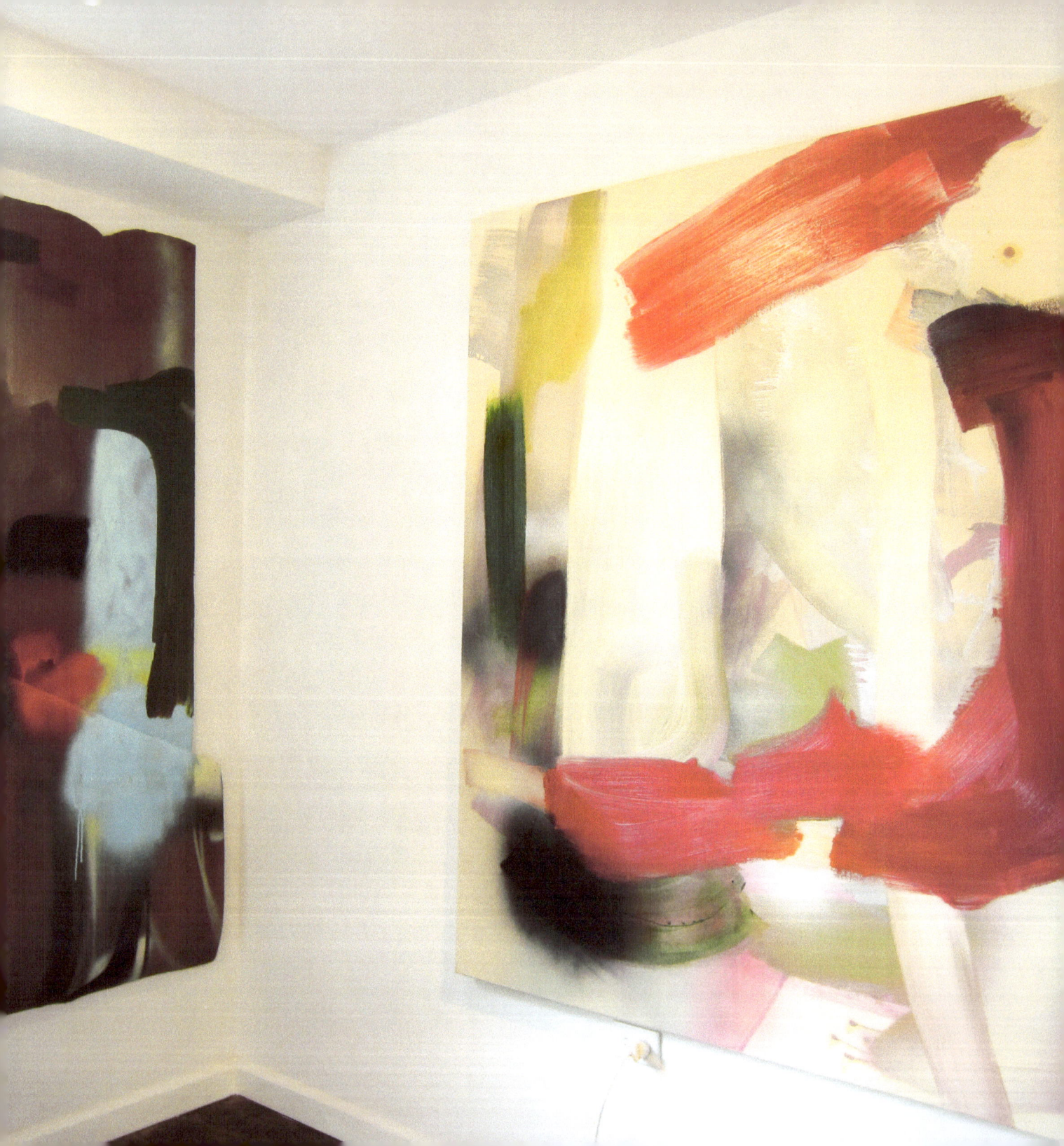

GLENN GARVER My paintings are a depiction of my perceptions, both conscious and subconscious. My work is not preconceived with preparatory steps such as sketches or studies, as these would only encumber. Rather, I experience the conception of each painting in the process of its creation. Each painting begins with the excitement of what will happen; some come quickly, others take the long way 'round, lingering and haunting until they come to completion.

Each canvas is singular, yet all have evolved from the paintings that preceded them. Over the past 25 years my work has transformed from representational to minimalist, to my current paintings. Yet there has always been a common thread, with the familiar feeling of clarity I experience while painting the basis for this commonality.

PAINTING 4, 2013, OIL AND SPRAYPAINT ON PLYWOOD, 74 IN. × 60 IN.

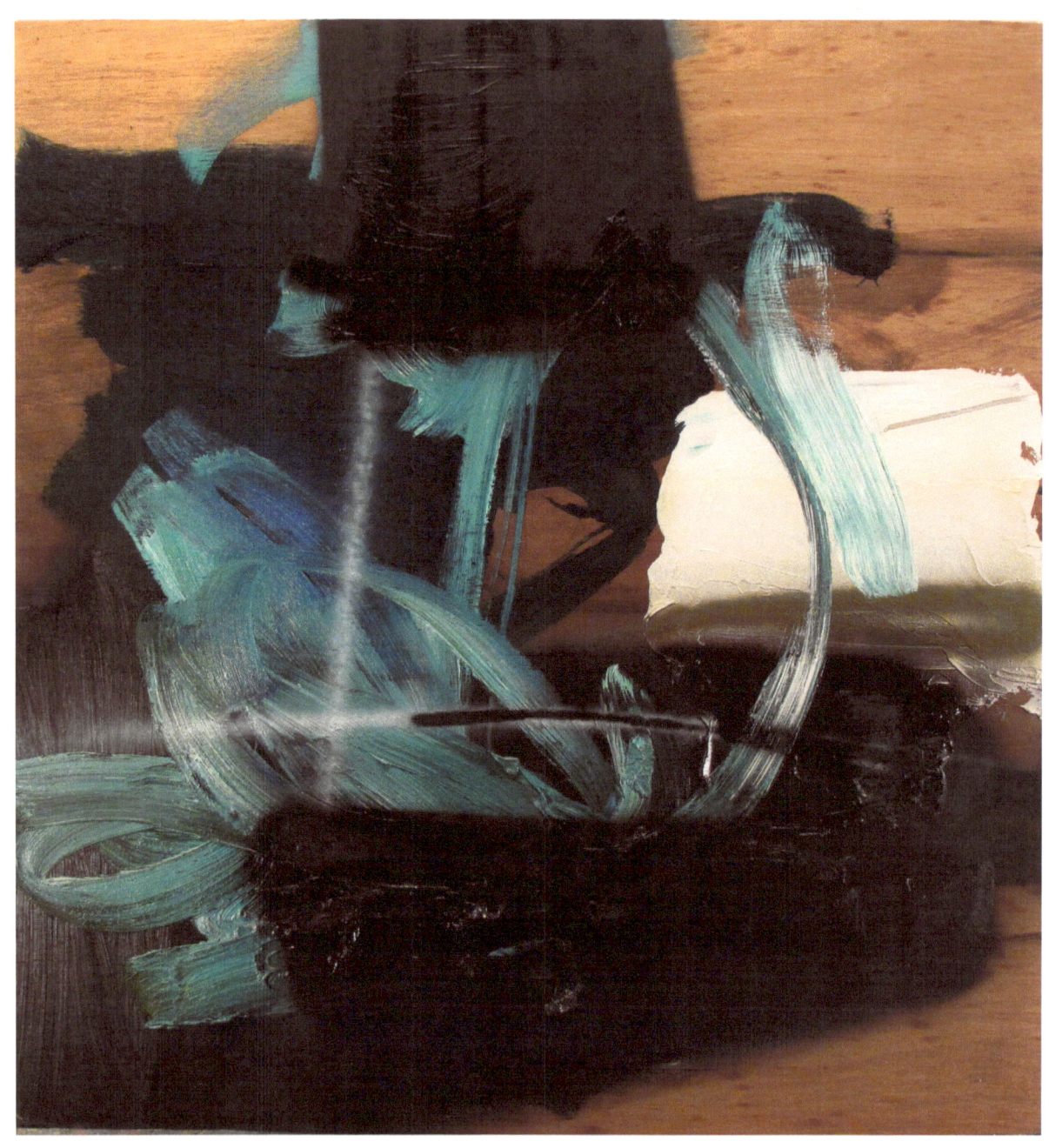

PAINTING I, 2013, OIL AND SPRAYPAINT ON PLYWOOD, 36 IN. × 38 IN.

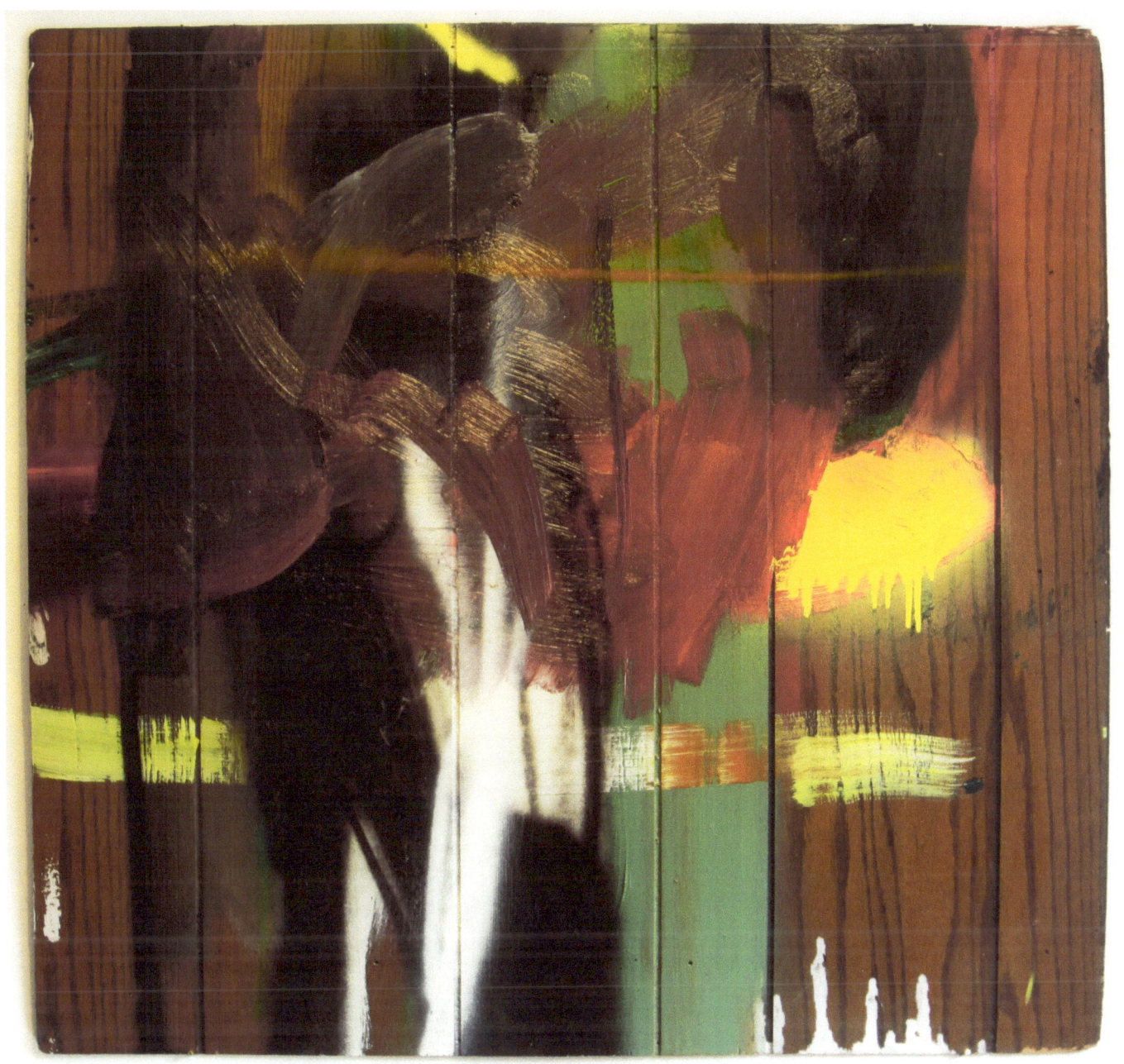

PAINTING 2, 2013, OIL AND SPRAYPAINT ON PANELING, 35 IN. × 34 IN.

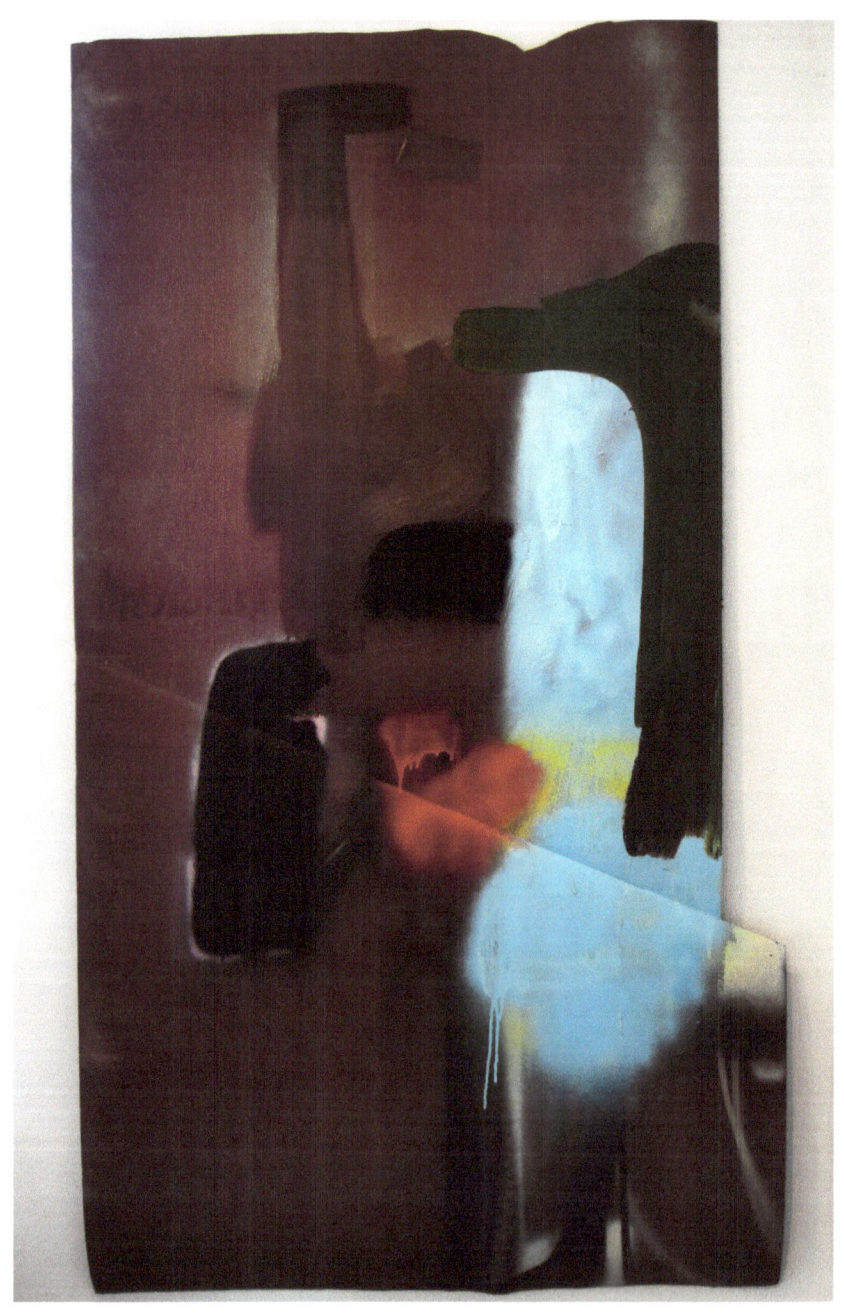

PAINTING 3, 2013, OIL AND SPRAYPAINT ON SANDPAPER, 75 IN. × 39 IN.

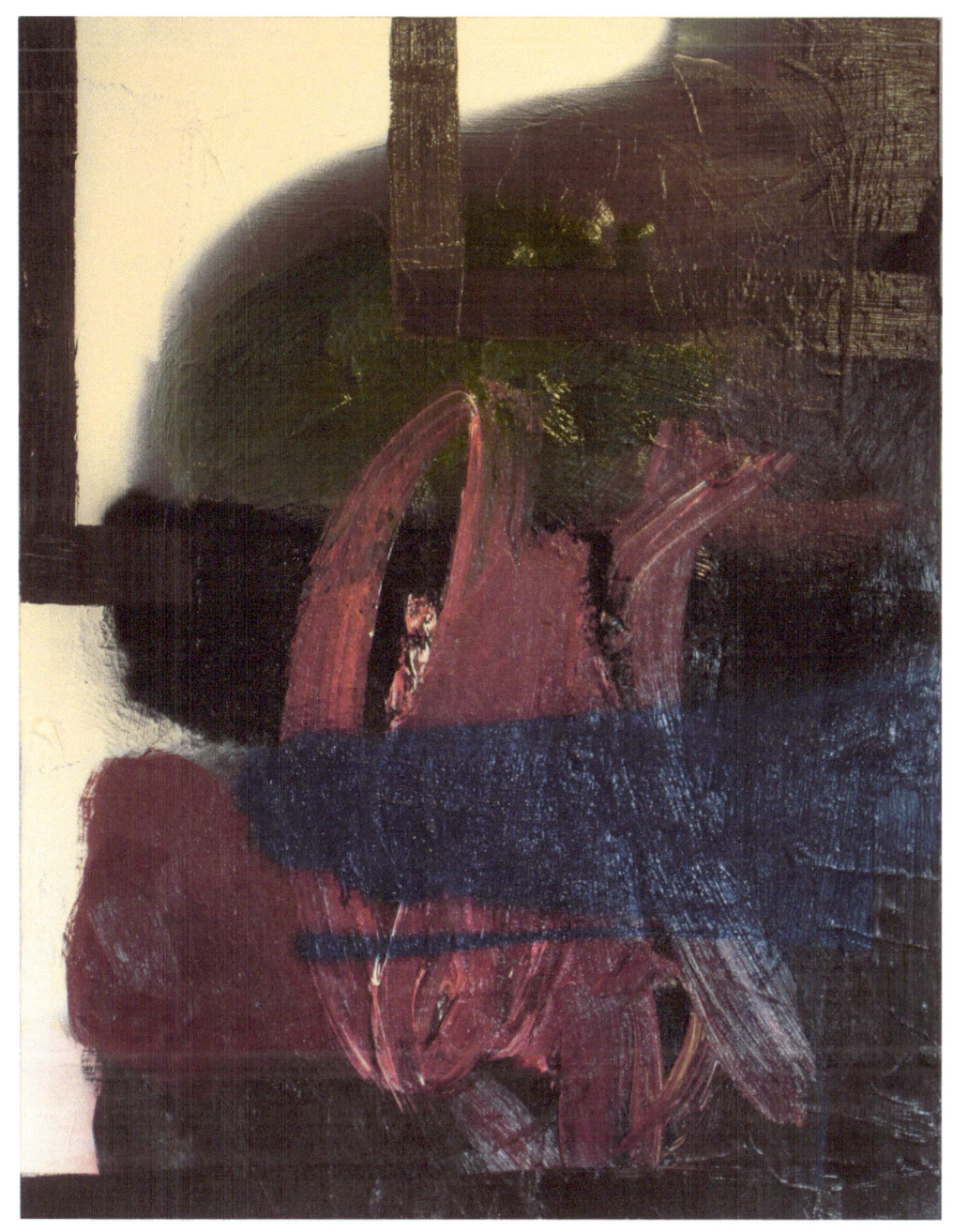

PAINTING 5, 2013, OIL AND SPRAYPAINT ON CANVAS, 38 IN. × 30 IN.

PAINTING 6, 2013, OIL AND SPRAYPAINT ON PAPER, 40 IN. × 26 IN.

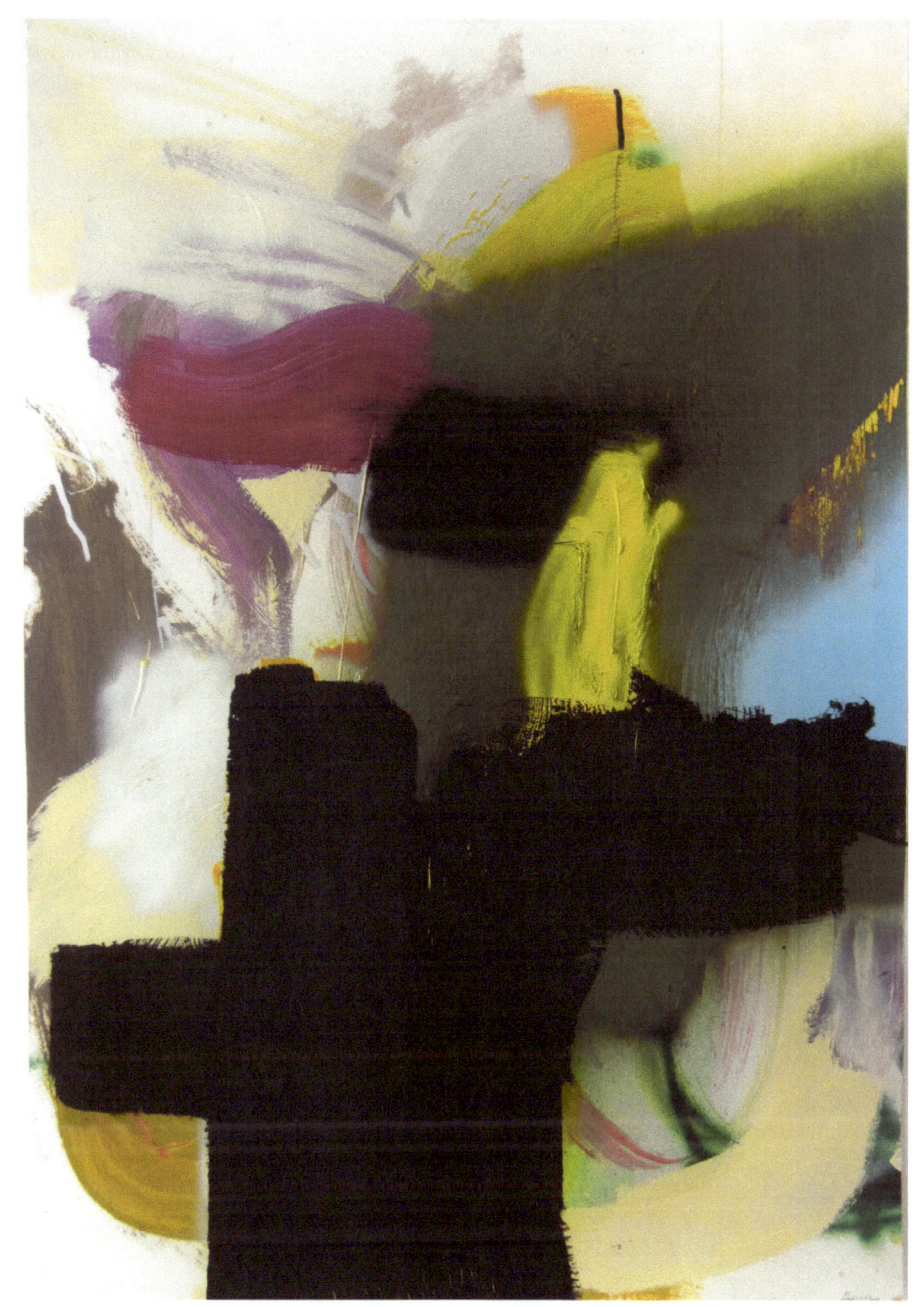

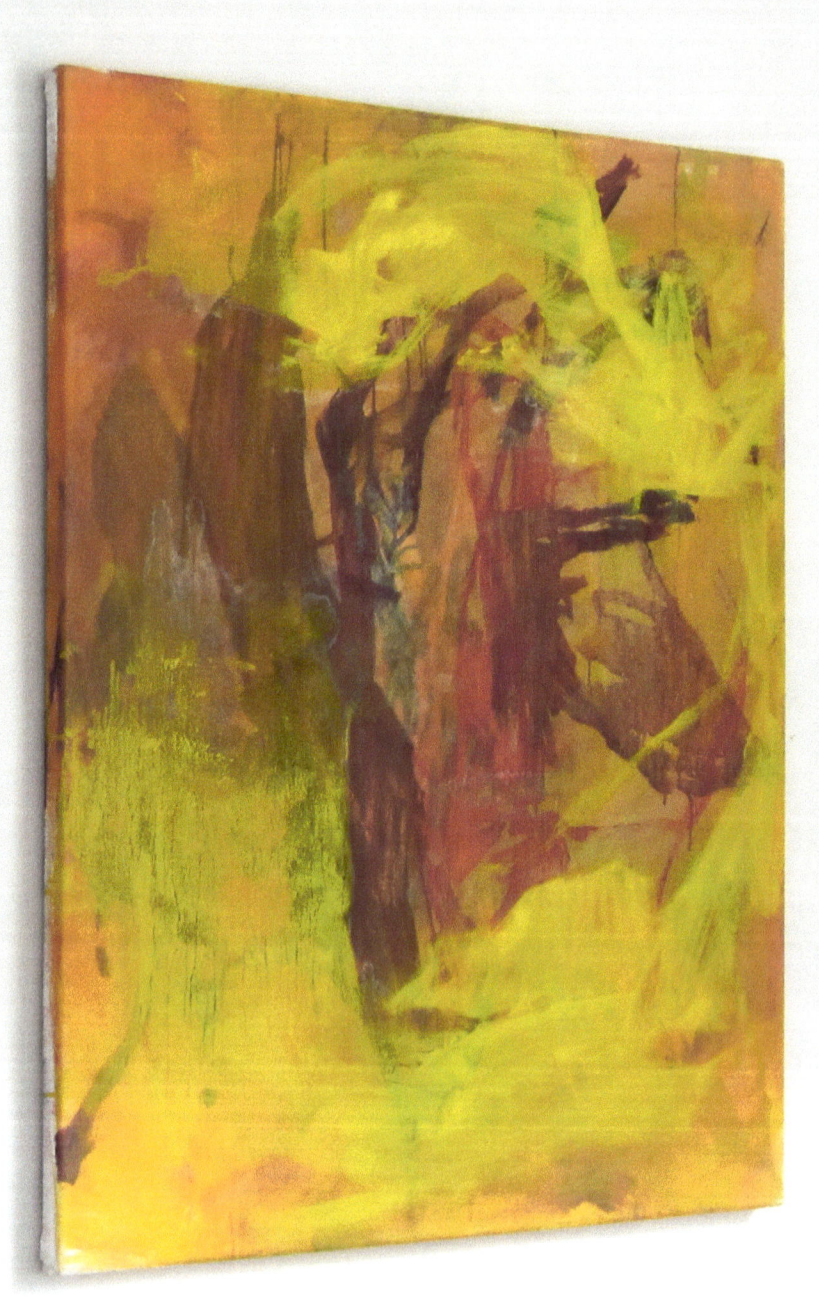

ELIZABETH GILFILEN   received a BFA from the University of Cincinnati, and a MFA from Virginia Commonwealth University. Awards include a Yaddo Residency, The Marie Walsh Sharpe Foundation Space Program, The Bronx Museum's AIM Program, the Alijra Emerge Fellowship 9, and a Gallery Aferro Studio Residency. Recently, she completed a printmaking residency at Oehme Graphics in Colorado, and was a Studio Immersion Project Fellow at the Robert Blackburn Printmaking Workshop in New York.

Her paintings and works on paper have been included in exhibitions at the Aldrich Contemporary Art Museum, the Islip Art Museum and Lehman College Gallery, among others. Solo exhibitions include the Hunterdon Art Museum, Clinton, NJ, 2012; Gallery Aferro, Newark, NJ, 2011; and John Davis Gallery, Hudson, NY, 2010. Her work has been published in *New American Paintings*; reviewed in *Two Coats of Paint*, *The Boston Globe* and *The New York Times*.

TRAP-VIEW, 2013, OIL ON CANVAS, 33 IN. × 29 IN.
ALL WORKS COURTESY OF FRED GIAMPIETRO GALLERY, NEW HAVEN

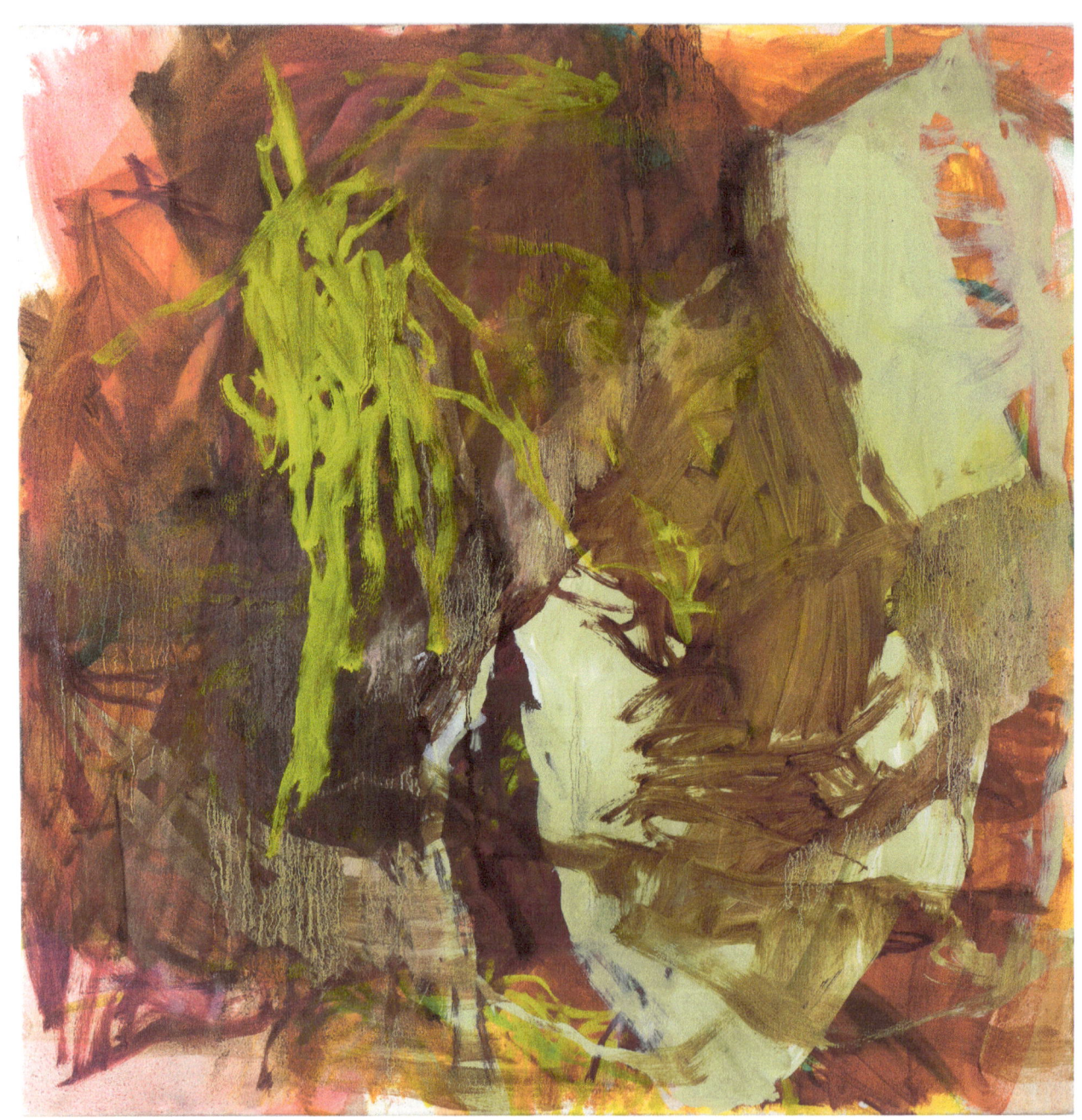

SEDIMENT, 2013, OIL ON CANVAS, 30 IN. × 30 IN.

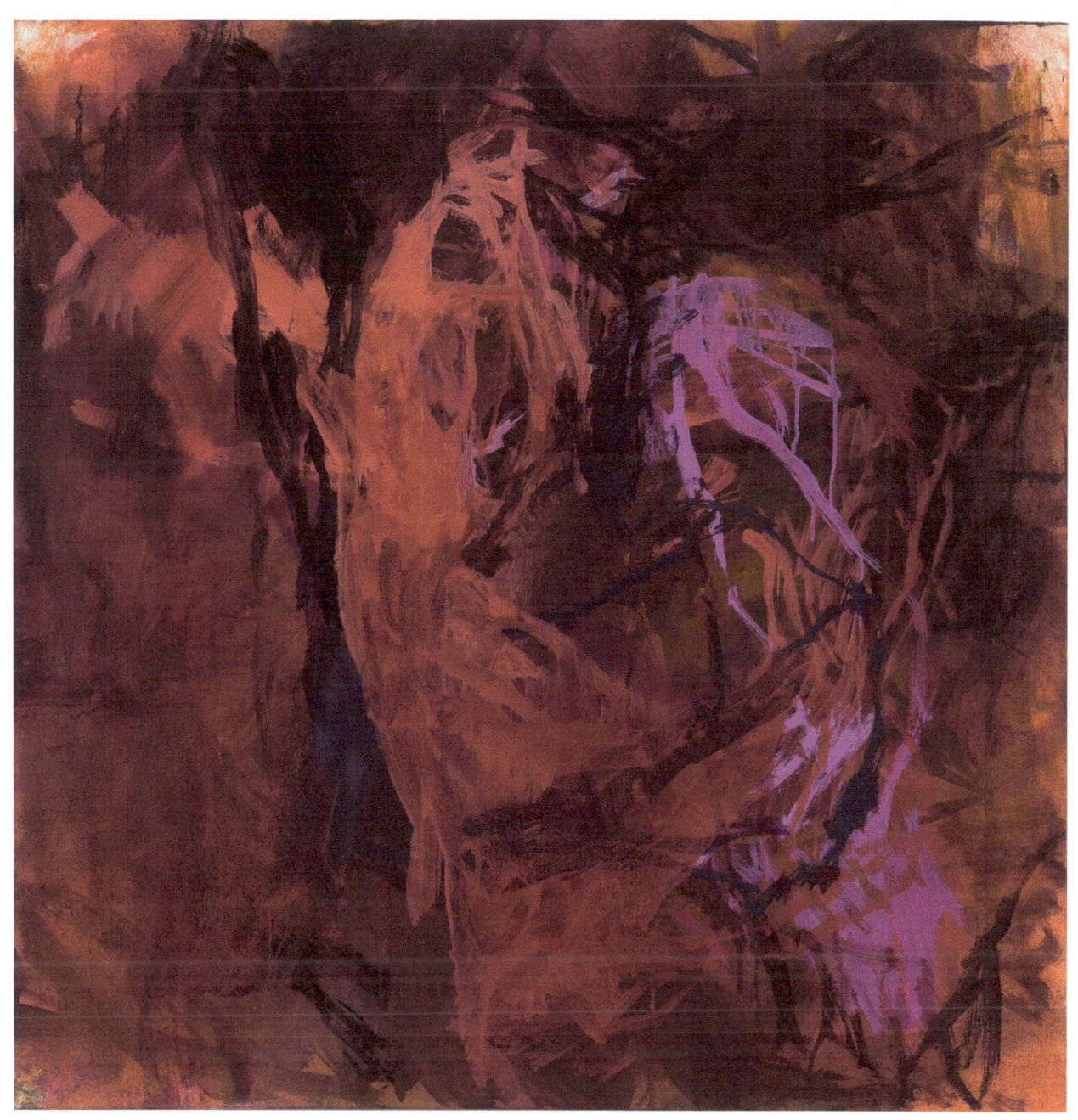

SWARM, 2013, OIL ON CANVAS, 30 IN. × 30 IN.

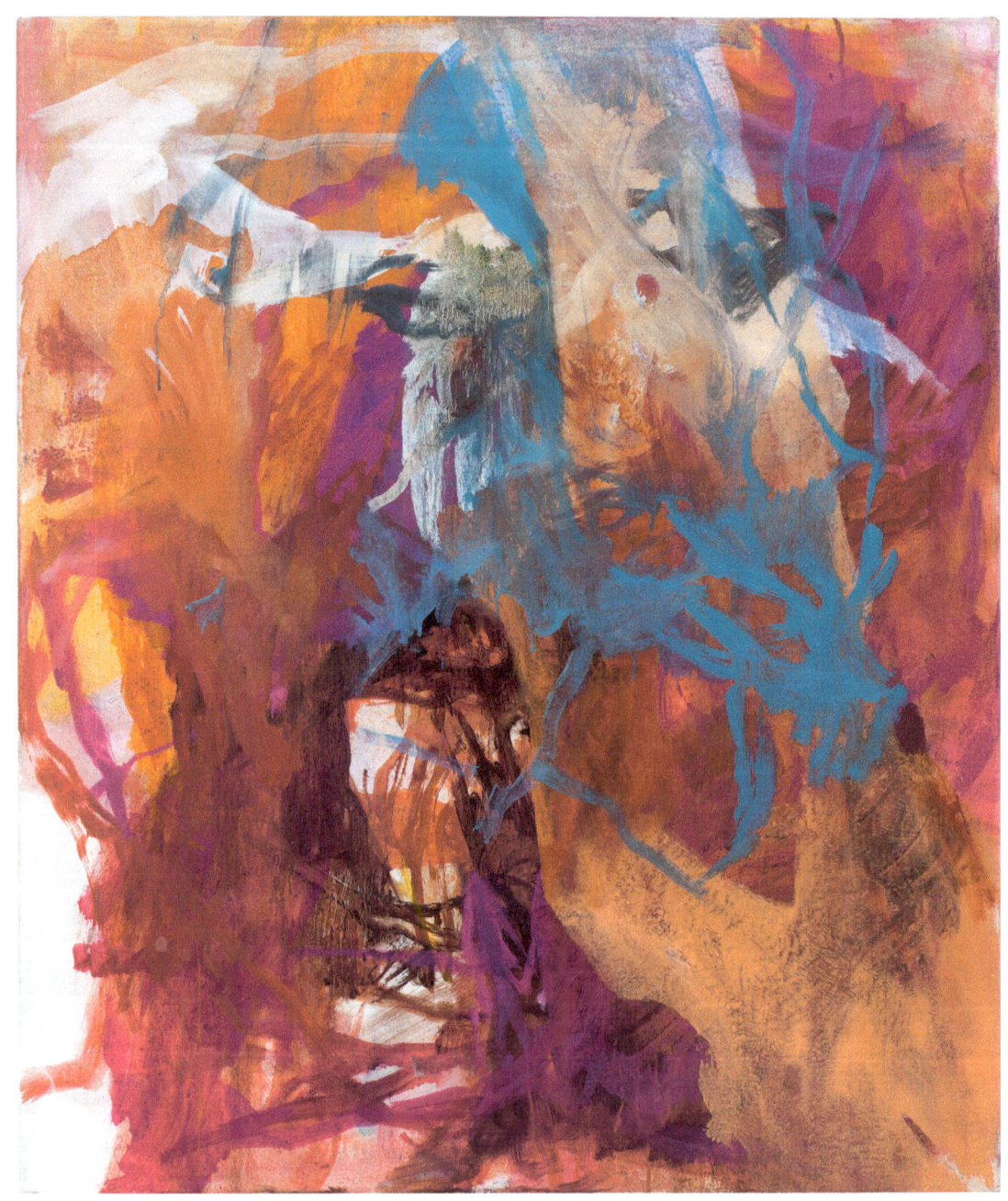

PURPLE IN BETWEEN, 2013, OIL ON CANVAS, 33 IN. × 29 IN.

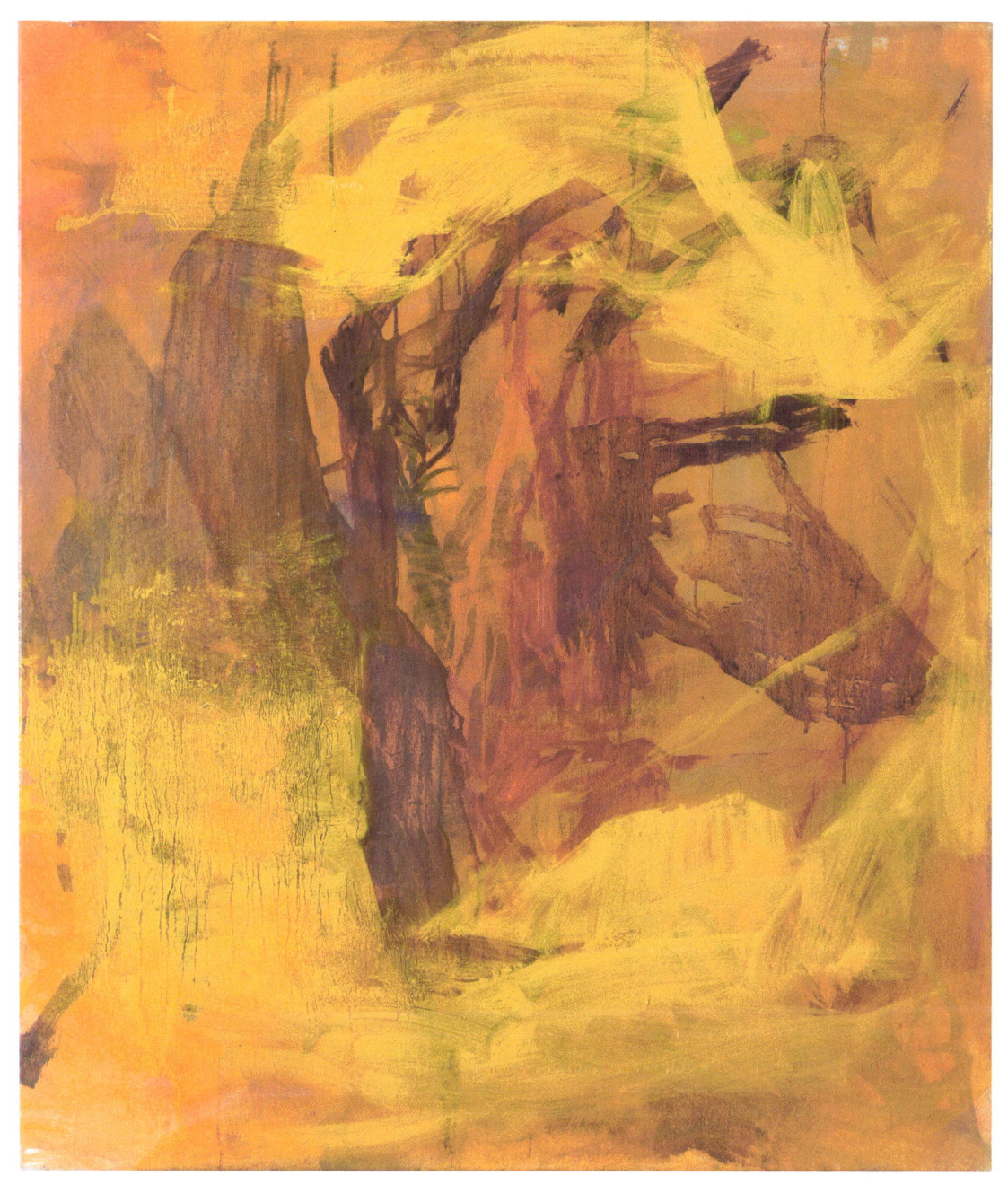

TRAP-VIEW, 2013, OIL ON CANVAS, 33 IN. × 29 IN.

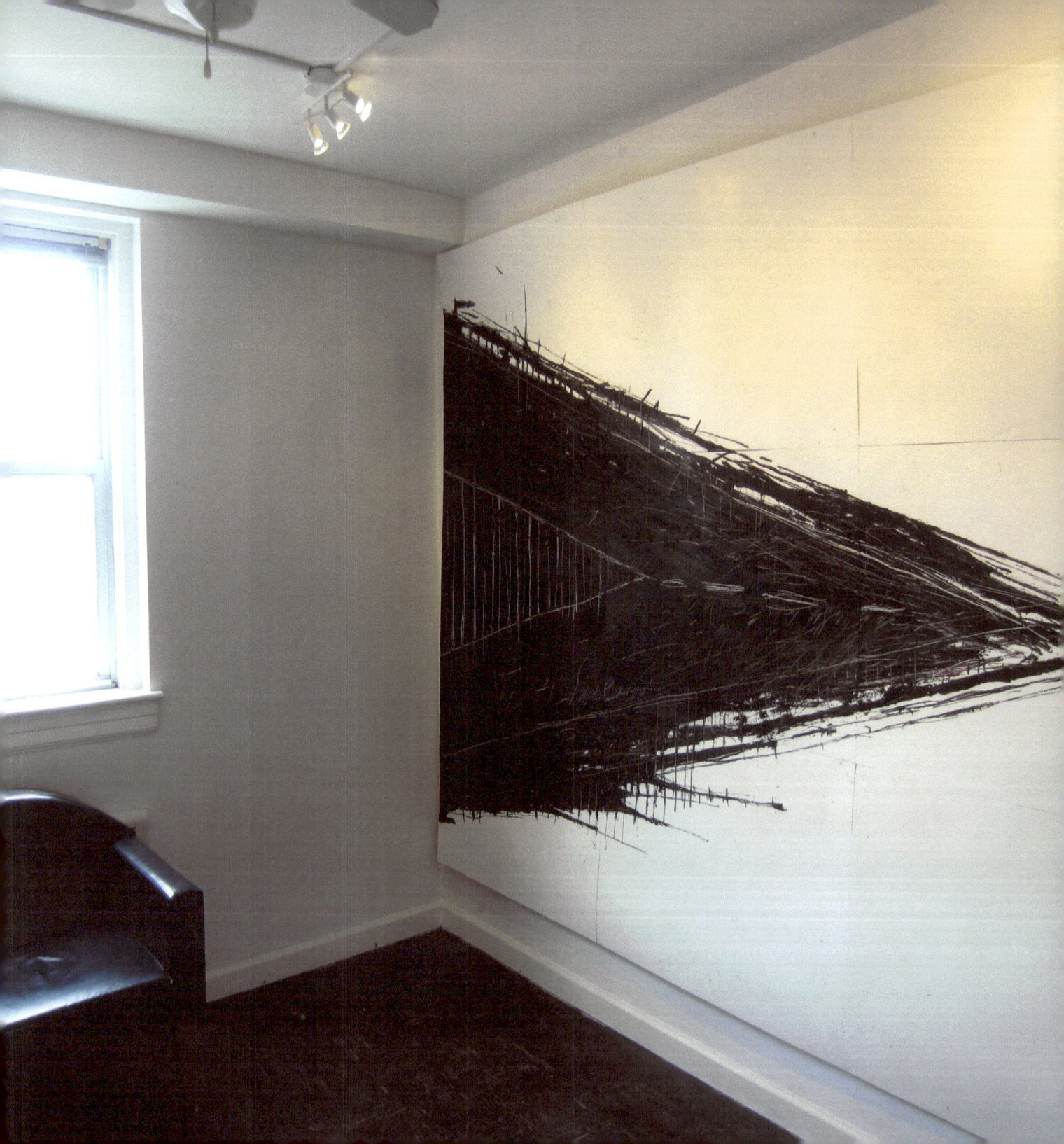

MARIA PAVLOVSKA   was born in Skopje, Macedonia (Former Yugoslavia). Her work has been featured around the globe in over 25 solo shows and more than 100 group international exhibitions including the Kunsthalle-Vienna and Kunsthalle-Krems (Austria), Gallery Lang (Vienna, Austria), Cite Internationale des Arts in Paris, Museum of Contemporary Art in Skopje, City House in Nurnberg (Germany), Station Gallery (Tribeca NY) Gallery MC (Midtown NY), Fernando Luis Alvarez Gallery (Connecticut), Viota Gallery (San Juan, Puerto Rico). Her work is held in private and public collections worldwide, including embassies, museums, galleries and libraries. Her artistic journey started at an early age, she was noticed as a one of Europe's promising young talents. She took up residencies in Paris, Vienna and Nuremberg until finally venturing in the United States. After her first solo in New York in 2007, she has lived and continued to been active in the New York art scene.

Critics have described her work as having "a strong personality" which "translates her topics of choice into pictorial language that demonstrates a quietly powerful eloquence". She has received praise from critics worldwide for her drawings and paintings with work that reflects painting as a battlefield, where light and darkness fight and the result is unpredictable, one sees the lightning bolts of ideas at work, as they are being worked out.

This sort of simultaneous image "process / result" dialectic lies frozen in space, stimulating the viewer to actively participate in the image creation themselves by way of investigation, inviting myriad readings within a given theme.

DIRECTION, 2013, OIL ON CARDBOARD, 80 IN. × 120 IN.

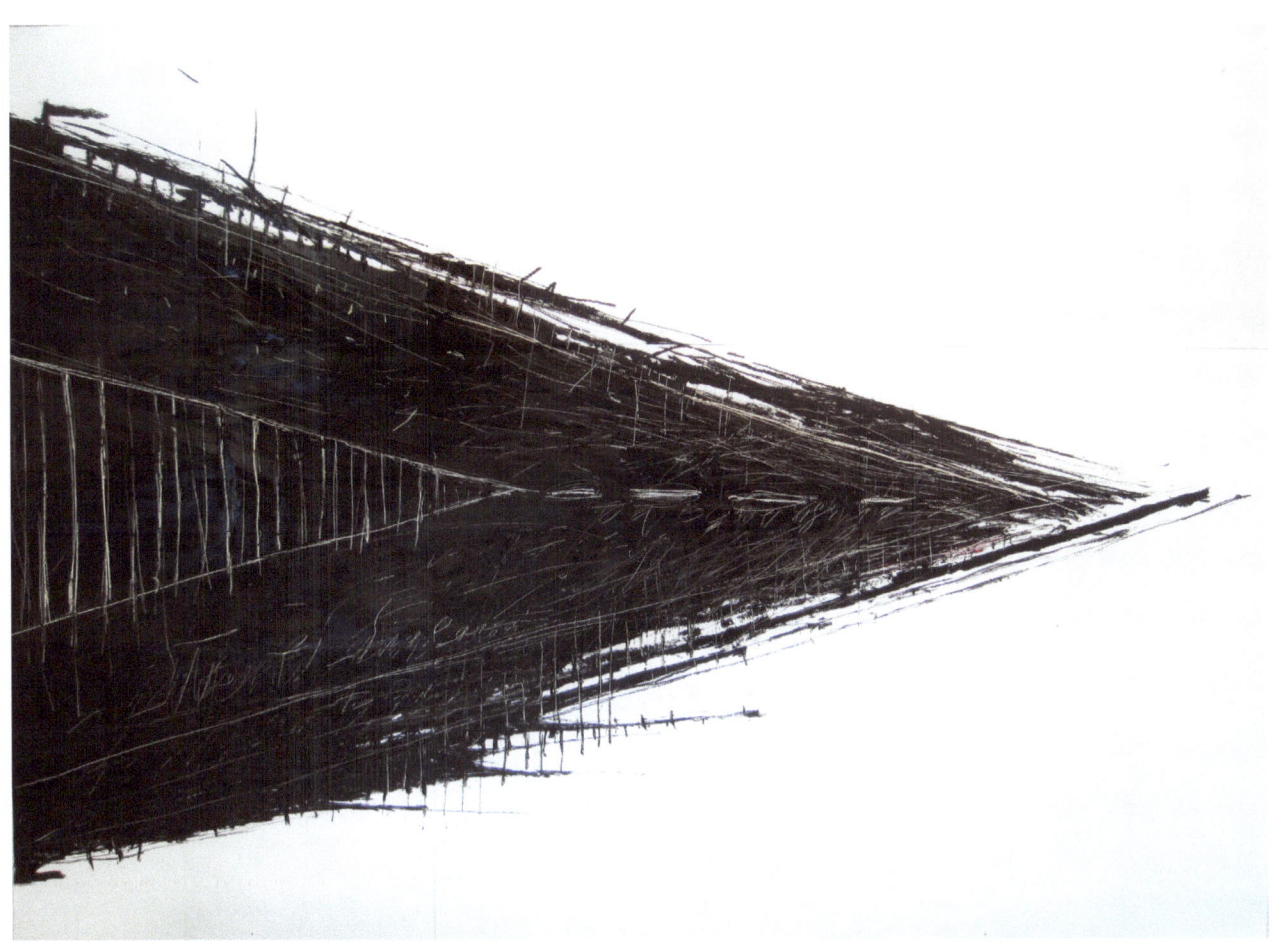

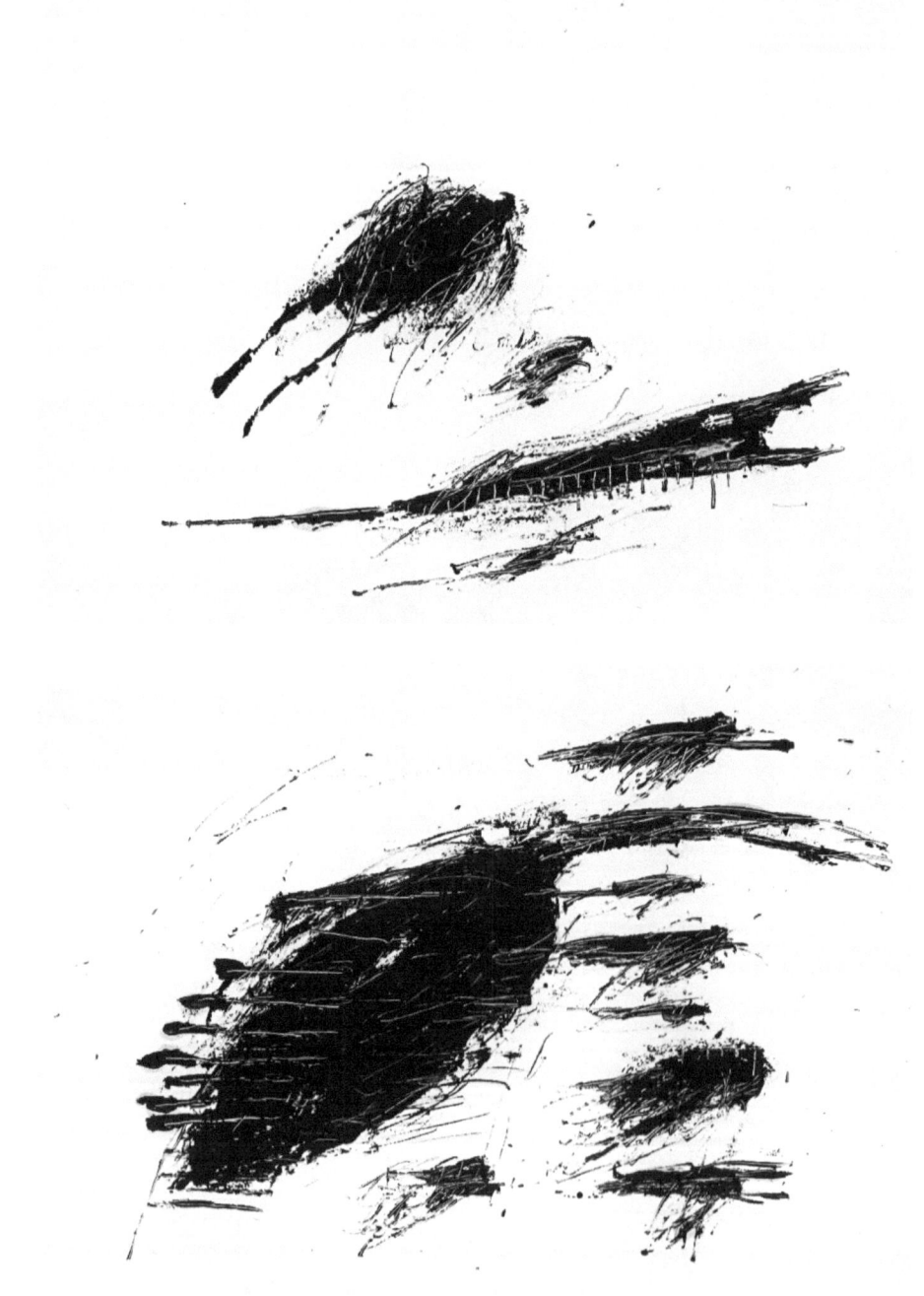

INTIMATE LANDSCAPE I [TOP], *INTIMATE LANDSCAPE II* [BOTTOM], 2007, OIL ON CARDBOARD, 27 IN. × 39 IN. EACH

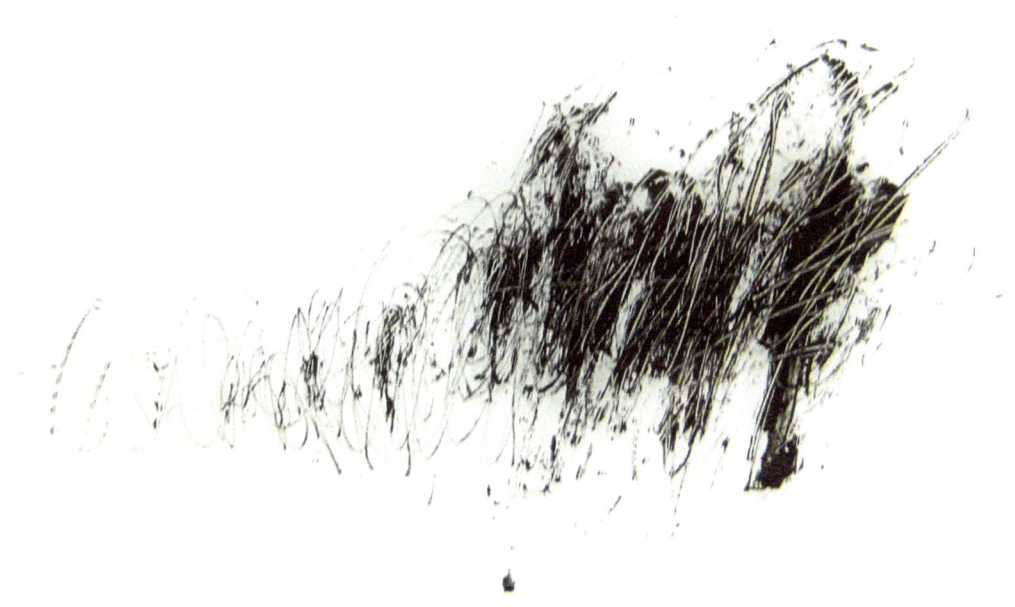

INTIMATE LANDSCAPE IV, 2007, OIL ON CARDBOARD, 20 IN. × 27 IN.

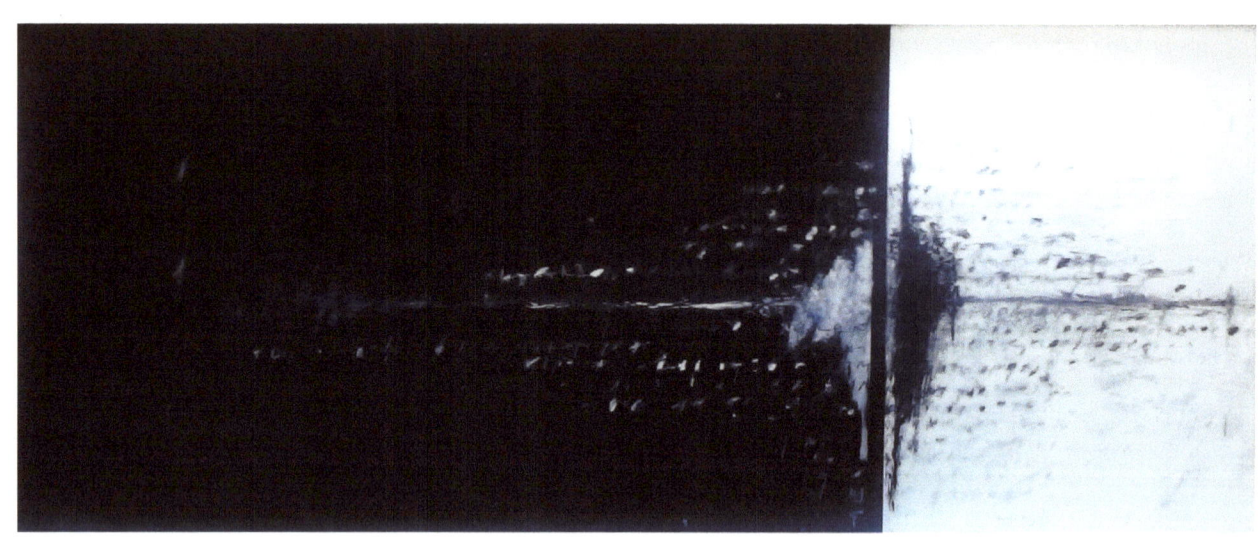

INDUSTRY OF THE SOUL I, 2012, OIL ON CARDBOARD, 10 IN. × 27 IN.

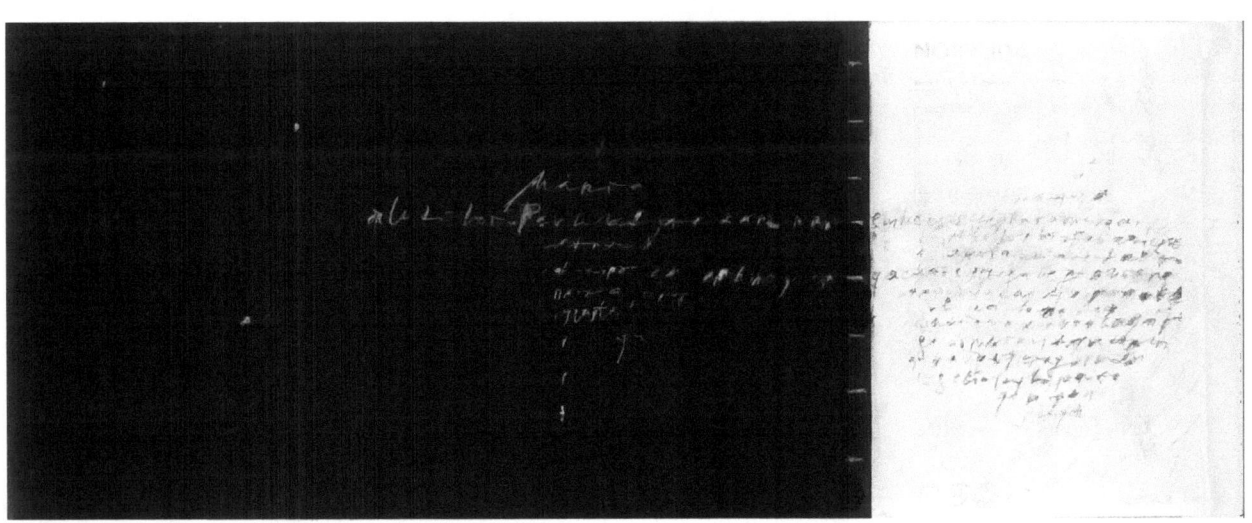

INDUSTRY OF THE SOUL II, 2012, OIL ON CARDBOARD, 10 IN. × 27 IN.

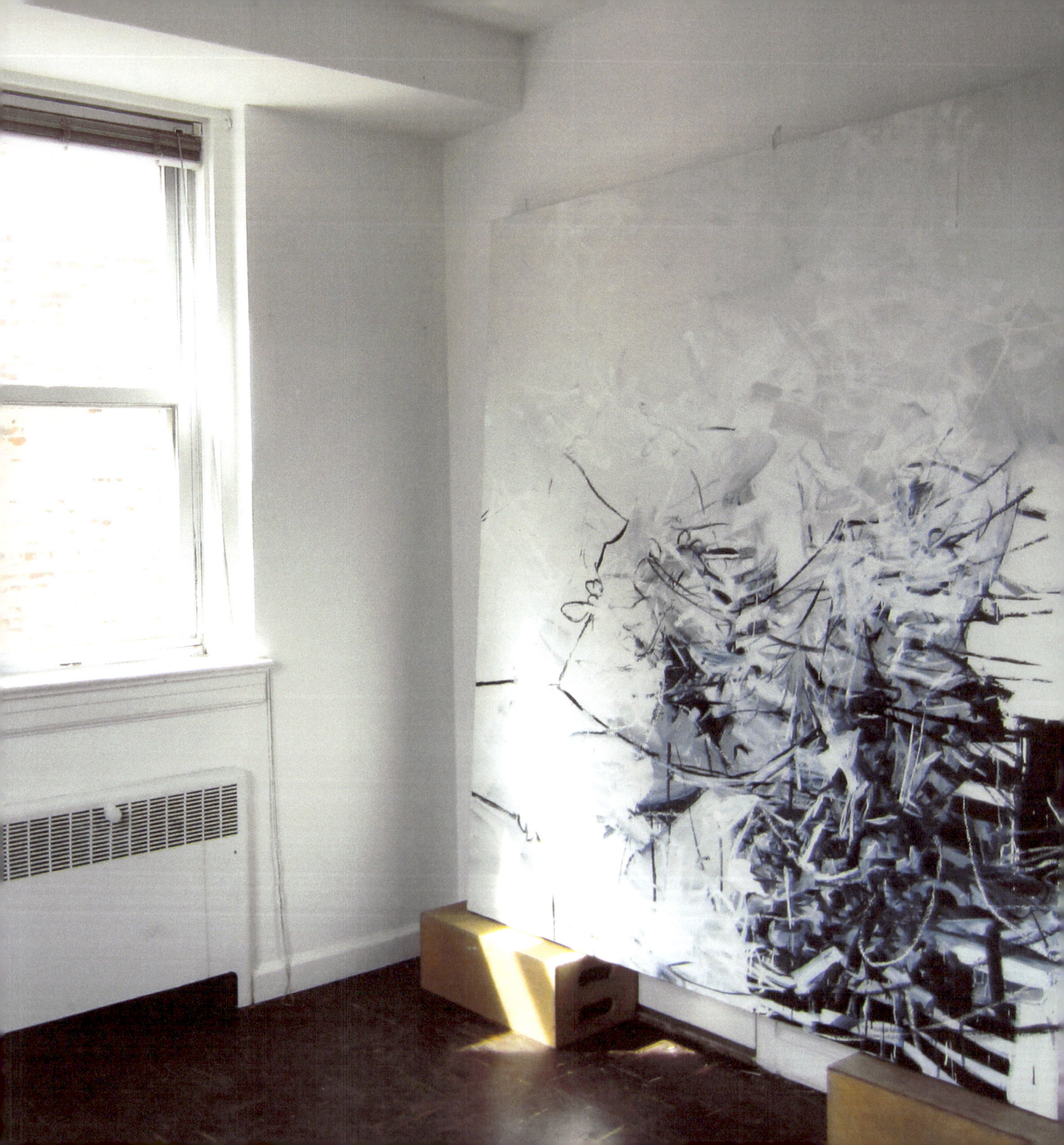

RAYMOND SAA "My work and the way I think about it have naturally evolved over the years.

There are many more aspects of myself that I can now recognize and accept; primarily 'myself 'and my 'work' are one and the same. My work is not 'about something' it is a reflection of me and therefore of what inspires me. The visual, auditory, and sensory minutiae that competes for daily attention is the inspiration to work. The way this is achieved is what my work is 'about'.

I am however very influenced by the resilience yet delicacy of botanical subjects particularly when it comes in direct conflict with urbanity. There is something inevitable but equally magical about a tender vine pushing its way through tarmacadam and enveloping a man-made structure. I hope my work conveys this organic aggression however abstractly or even metaphorically it may be viewed. My thoughts on my own artwork are that by its very nature it becomes a deeply personal reflection of the artist, i.e. me that is to be read or shared by the viewer."

UNTITLED, 2011, OIL ON CANVAS, 72 IN. × 60 IN.

UNTITLED, 2011, OIL ON CANVAS, 72 IN. × 60 IN.

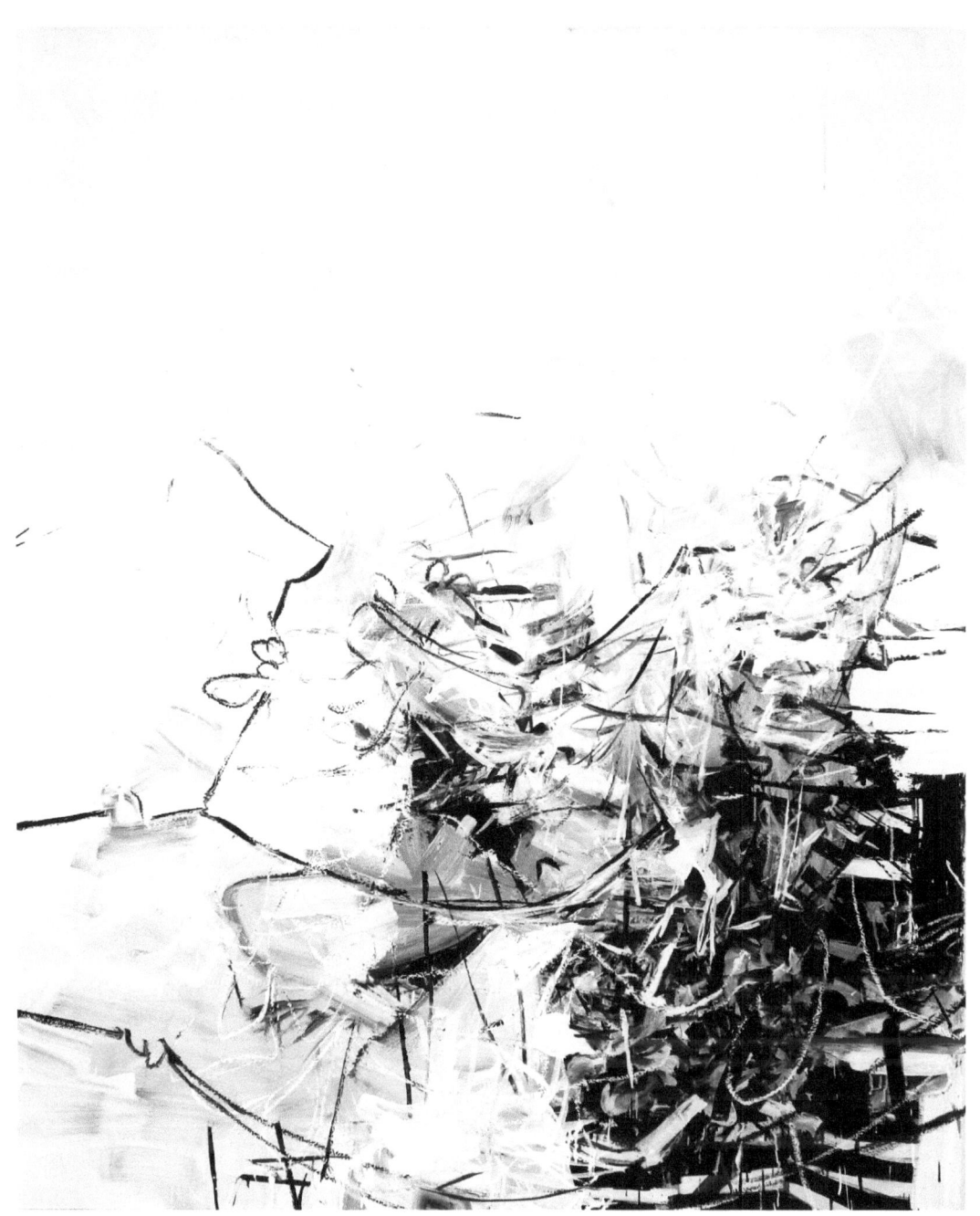

UNTITLED, 2011, OIL ON CANVAS, 60 IN. × 48 IN.

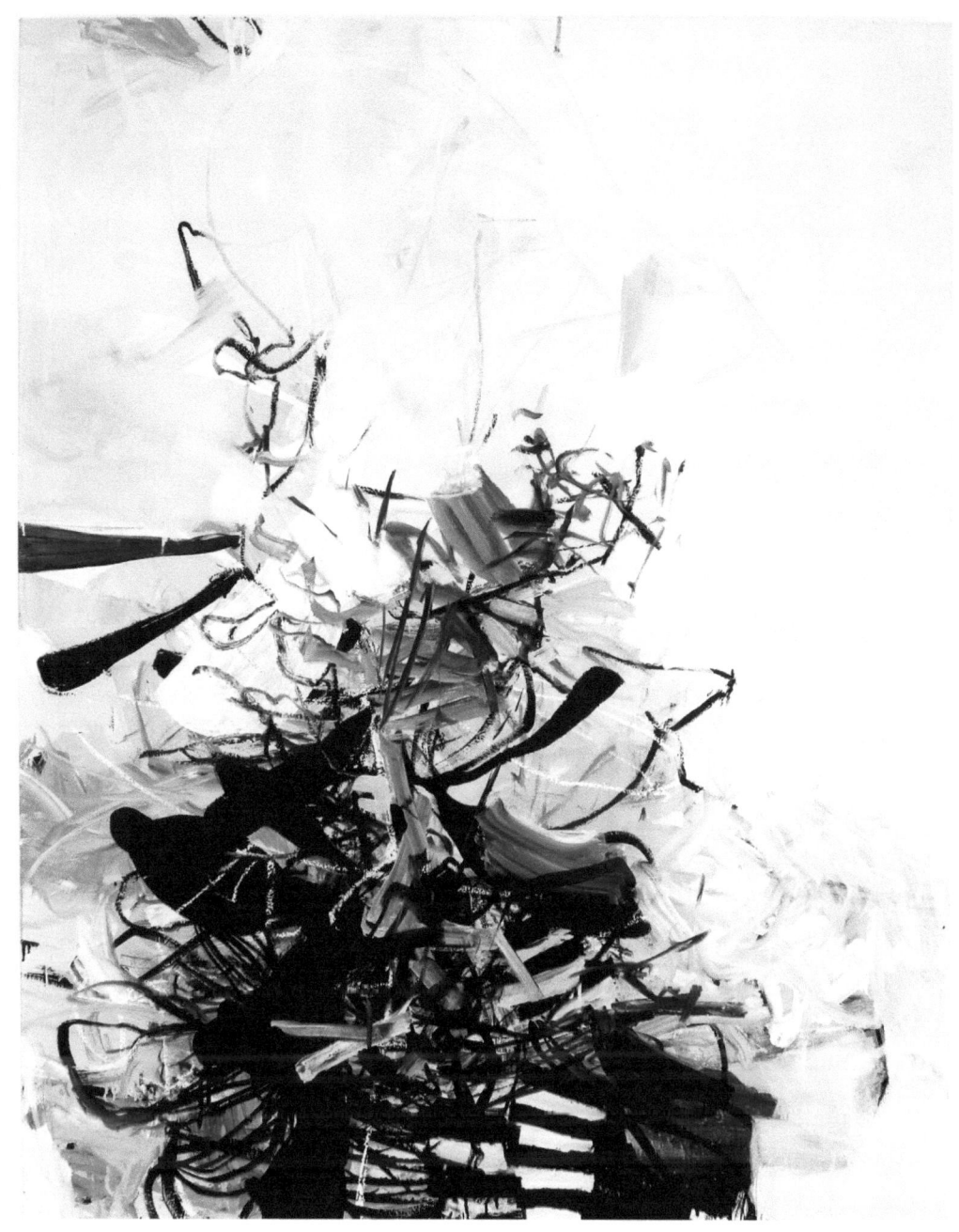

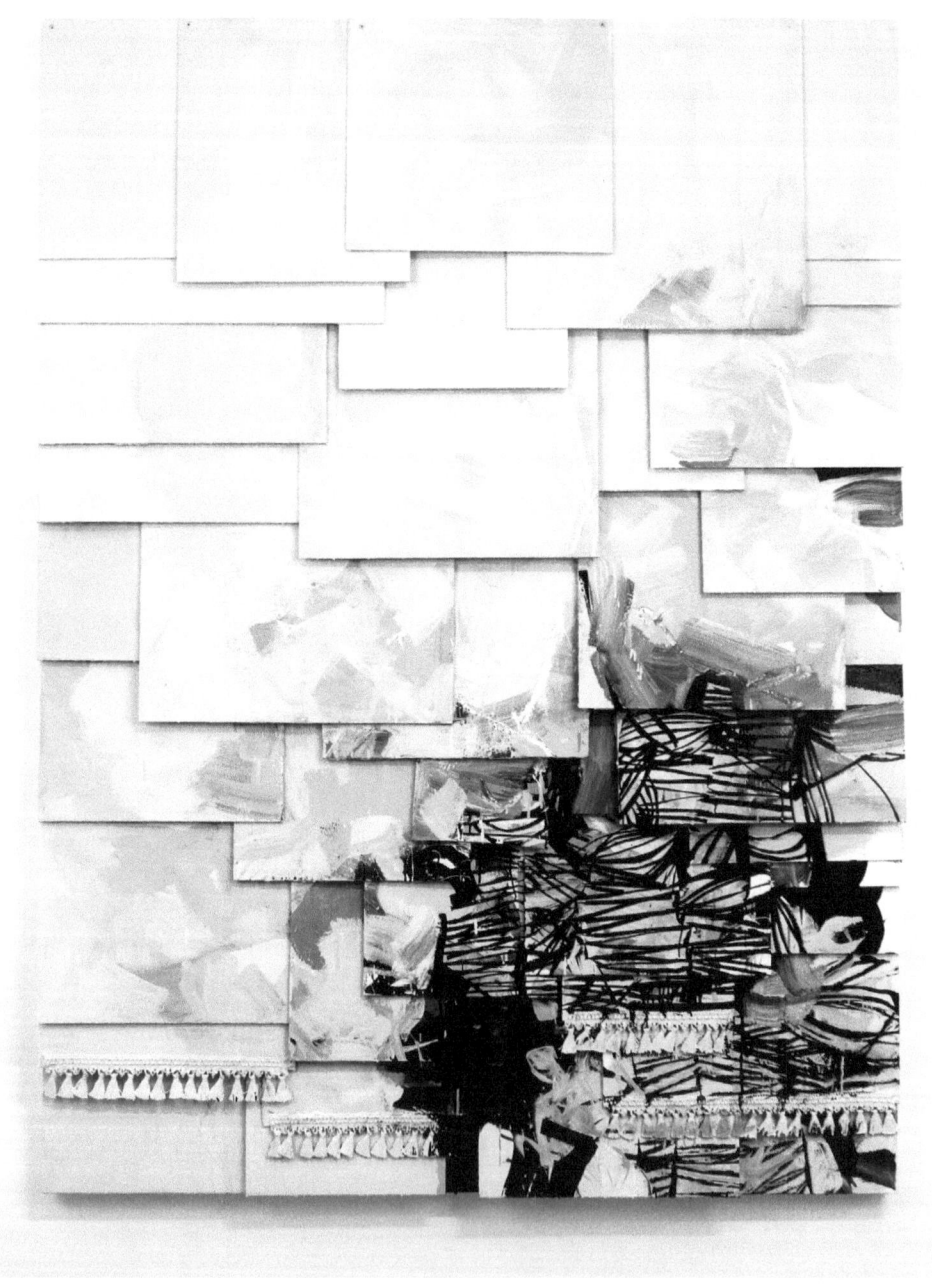

UNTITLED, 2011, OIL ON WOOD, 80 IN. × 60 IN.

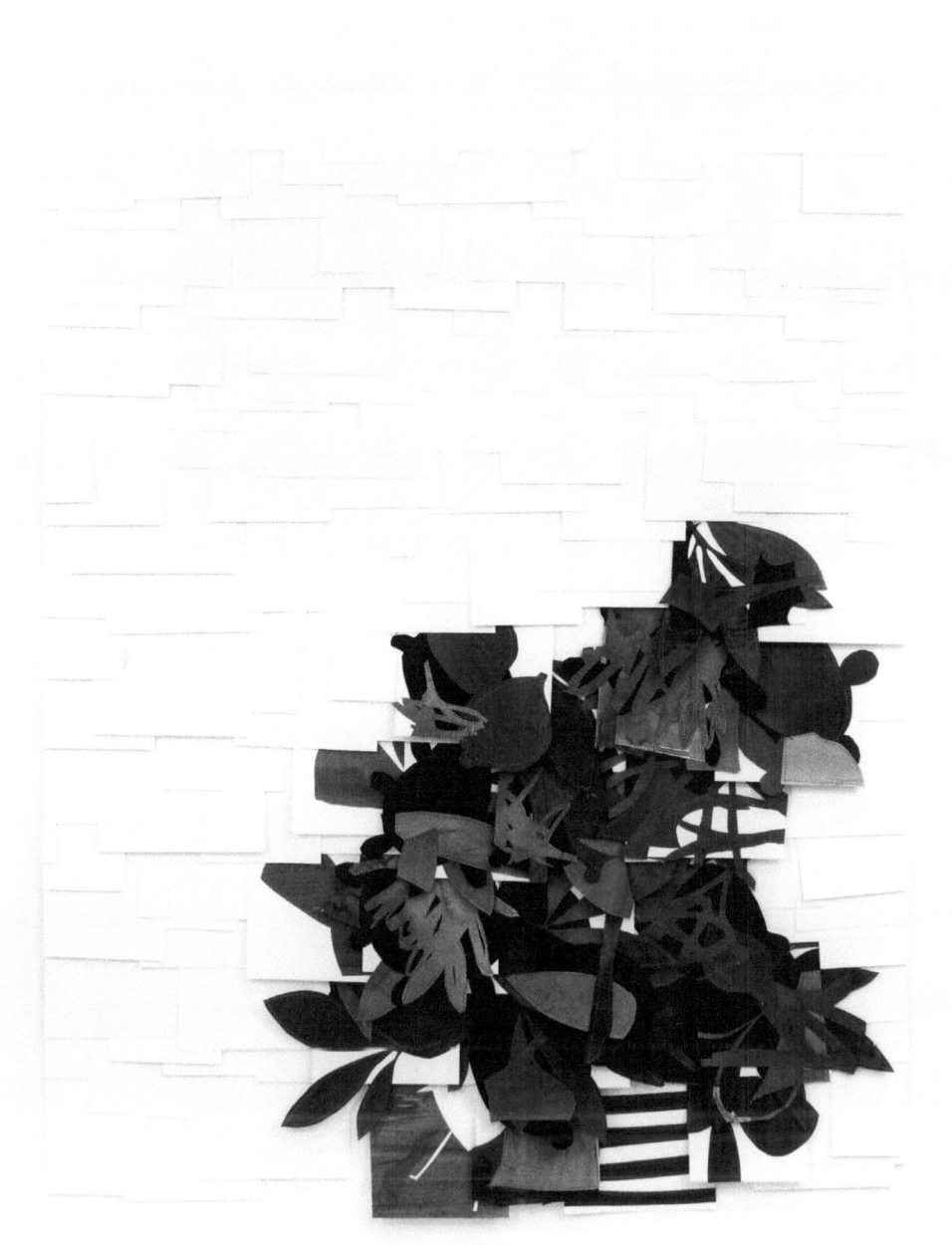

UNTITLED, 2011, GOUACHE COLLAGE ON SEWN PAPER, 51.5 IN. × 41 IN. FRAMED

This program is made possible in part by funds from the New Jersey State Council on the Arts / Department of State, a partner agency of the National Endowment for the Arts, administered by the Hudson County Office of Cultural and Heritage Affairs, Thomas A DeGise, County Executive, and the Board of Chosen Freeholders.

Published in conjunction with the exhibition:

PICTURES of EVERYTHING ABSTRACT PAINTING NOW

March 27—May 4, 2014

VICTORY HALL DRAWING ROOMS

180 GRAND ST JERSEY CITY
WWW.DRAWINGROOMS.ORG
HOURS: THURSDAY & FRIDAY 4–7 PM,
SATURDAY & SUNDAY 2–6 PM

SBN-13: 978-0692201923
ISBN-10: 0692201920

Edited by Jim Pustorino
Designed by Eileen Boxer

VICTORY HALL PRESS is a division of Victory Hall Inc., a not-for-profit arts organization producing exhibitions, events, education programs, public projects and publications, based in the NJ/NY metro area.

Visit our website at www.victoryhallpress.org
Contact us at victoryhall1@msn.com

NEW DRAWING presents series of innovative, current images from artists whose work explores and expands the visual and conceptual language of drawing. Other books in the Series include:

Ibou Ndoye: *Forms of Faces*

Ibou Ndoye: *Taarou Adaa*

Jill Scipione: *Skullnotebook*

Carl Vierow: *Detective at Red Castle Pier and Other Drawings*

James Pustorino: *Universechild*

Hector G Romero: *Last Coast Blues*

Cheryl Gross: *Drawings from the Z Factor*

www.ingramcontent.com/pod-product-compliance
Lightning Source LLC
Chambersburg PA
CBHW050740180526
45159CB00003B/1290